WONDER
AND
WORSHIP

ADRIAN ROGERS

innovo
PUBLISHING.COM

Published by Innovo Publishing, LLC
www.innovopublishing.com
1-888-546-2111

Providing Full-Service Publishing Services for Christian Authors, Artists & Ministries:
Books, eBooks, Audiobooks, Music, Screenplays, Film & Curricula

Wonder & Worship
Adrian Rogers

We gratefully acknowledge the help of the following people in the creation of
Wonder & Worship:

Melanie Redd, General Editor
Deborah Wade, Contributing Editor
Brandi Hayes, Contributing Editor

ISBN: 978-1-61314-853-2

Cover Design: Jeff Hatcher & Innovo Publishing LLC
Interior Layout: Houseal Creative & Innovo Publishing, LLC
Printed in the United States of America
U.S. Printing History
First Edition: 2022

Has God called you to create a Christian book, eBook, audiobook, music album,
screenplay, film, or curricula? If so, visit the ChristianPublishingPortal.com to learn
how to accomplish your calling with excellence. Learn to do everything yourself, or
hire trusted Christian Experts from our Marketplace to help.

Guide to Studying
Your Bible

FIVE SIMPLE STEPS FROM
PASTOR ADRIAN ROGERS

PRAY OVER IT

Begin with prayer. Ask
for God's cleansing and
the ability to receive what
He wants to teach you.

PONDER IT

What did it mean **then**?
What does it mean **now**?
What does it mean **to me**?

PUT IT IN WRITING

Write down what
**the Holy Spirit is
revealing** to you.

PRACTICE IT

Find ways you can **incorporate
the truths** you've just been
shown into your own life.

PROCLAIM IT

Contemplate ways to
share the knowledge
God has given you.

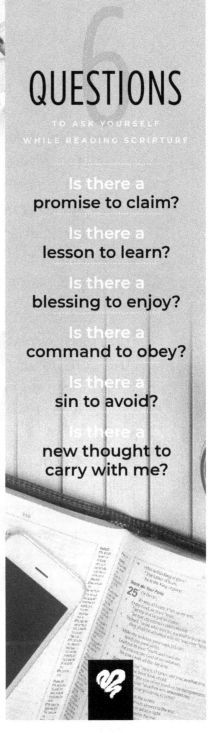

QUESTIONS

TO ASK YOURSELF
WHILE READING SCRIPTURE

Is there a
promise to claim?

Is there a
lesson to learn?

Is there a
blessing to enjoy?

Is there a
command to obey?

Is there a
sin to avoid?

Is there a
new thought to
carry with me?

May we never come to the
place where the joy and
wonder go out of our worship.
We are to worship God with
enthusiasm, not weariness.
In fact, the word *enthusiasm* has
the word *Theos* (God) at its root.

We should be excited—
enthousiasmos—about serving
the Lord Jesus Christ. Every day
should become sweeter.

———

May our praise rise to
Heaven like sweet incense, an
offering worthy of our God—
the Great King.

ADRIAN ROGERS

Why "Wonder & Worship"?

Our highest privilege as Christians is to know and enjoy God's presence. Pastor Adrian Rogers taught that we are best able to enjoy this privilege when we recognize God's nature, reverence His name, and respect His nobility.

When we recognize Him as our Father, we honor Him, give Him weight in our thinking, and take Him seriously. When we realize He is our master, we "fear" Him appropriately—not a sick trepidation but, as Pastor Rogers said, "love on its knees."

We reverence the name of God because His name represents His character. Reverence means more than refusing to use swear words. "Profanity," Pastor Rogers said, "is when you use the name of God and you don't mean it. You sing His name and you're thinking about something else. It's an insult to Almighty God." Instead we are to bring our whole hearts—the very best of who we are—to worship Him.

Respecting the nobility of God will help us recognize His presence in our worship. "If we knew that the President or an earthly king planned to visit," Pastor Rogers mused, we would: "make sure to be there, sing with more feeling, engage mentally, and focus on our honored guest." There would be "a buzz of excitement in the air."

We hope that's where this book takes you. We've gathered some of Pastor Rogers' best thoughts about getting right with God so we can rediscover the true wonder of worship. God is present in our worship whether we are alone in quiet time, with a group, or at a large church gathering.

The King of kings is in our midst.

Lord, speak to my heart as I read today and show me how to know you more.

> The heavens declare the glory of God; and the firmament shows His handiwork. Day unto day utters speech, and night unto night reveals knowledge. There is no speech nor language where their voice is not heard. Their line has gone out through all the earth, and their words to the end of the world.
>
> **PSALM 19:1-4**

Did you know that you can know God personally? You don't have to guess about Him. And that's so very important. Truly, to know Him is to trust Him, to trust Him is to obey Him, and to obey Him is to be blessed.

How can you know God? Well, the nineteenth Psalm gives us some ways in which God speaks to us. And we don't have to guess about it. There can be no stutter, no stammer, no apology, and no equivocation. You can know God personally, intimately, assuredly.

To begin with, God speaks to us through the convincing Word of God in the heavens. In Psalm 19, we are told that God's convincing Word is in the heavens. As you look up into the starry night, as you see the vast Universe that Almighty God has created, you can know that there is a God. Someone formed and fashioned all of those planets, stars, and skies.

How long has it been since you looked up at night to see the starry skies? We get so busy and forget to look up. However, to look up and see the millions and billions of stars is to be reminded that we have a Creator. Looking up into the heavens will strengthen our faith and encourage us that we have a Heavenly Father who loves us and wants to have a personal relationship with us.

Take a few minutes and look up today, because "The heavens declare the glory of God, and the firmament shows His handiwork."

APPLICATION

When was the last time you went out at night and looked up at the stars? Why not try looking up tonight or on the next clear night? How do you think this might encourage your faith?

How does creation remind you of your Creator? Which parts of creation most encourage your faith in God—the ocean, the mountains, the stars, a quiet stream?

Would you like to grow closer to the Lord right now? Why not write out a prayer about your desire for God, sharing your heart in the space below?

As I study today, teach me more about Your power and might!

2

The heavens declare the glory of God; and the firmament shows His handiwork. Day unto day utters speech, and night unto night reveals knowledge. There is no speech nor language where their voice is not heard. Their line has gone out through all the earth, and their words to the end of the world.

PSALM 19:1-4

Someone once said, "God stepped from behind the curtain of nowhere and stood upon the platform of nothing and spoke a world into existence." (author unknown)

Did you know that a person can't create anything? No man has ever created a single thing. We talk about human beings with creativity. Indeed, all you can do is rearrange what God has already created. God created in one great act everything. God is the one who is behind all things.

Light travels at 186,282 miles per second. How fast is that? If you were to hijack a light beam and go to the moon, you could be there in about two seconds. At the speed of light, you would have to travel four and one-half years to get to the nearest star. To travel out to the rim of our known Universe, traveling at the speed of light, you would have to travel for ten billion years. Who made all of this? God did!

Also, we can consider the intricacies of God's creation. The smallest unit of human life is the cell. There are approximately three billion cells in your body. Some have described our cells as being more complicated than a huge metropolitan city.

Whether you look inward or whether you look outward, you see the vastness or the minuteness of His creation. It is true that "The heavens declare the glory of God, and the firmament shows His handiwork."

APPLICATION

When you think about the speed of light and the way God created the planets, how does this impact you? How great is God to you?

....

....

....

....

As you consider the intricacies of God's creation, what are your thoughts? Are you encouraged knowing that God has a great interest in the tiny details of our lives?

....

....

....

....

Why not write out a prayer to God as you close your devotional time today? Share your thoughts with the Lord below.

....

....

....

....

....

....

Open my heart to see and understand more of Your goodness and glory.

3

> The heavens declare the glory of God; and the firmament shows His handiwork. Day unto day utters speech, and night unto night reveals knowledge. There is no speech nor language where their voice is not heard. Their line has gone out through all the earth, and their words to the end of the world.
>
> **PSALM 19:1-4**

Did you know that creation not only displays God's glory and God's greatness but also shows us His goodness? God is good. And He is good to us.

There is a fixed order in the Universe. Night and day. Day and night. It is God who daily loads us with benefits. Indeed, His mercies are new every single morning. Every day, every human has the opportunity to see God call the sun to rise, cross the skies, and set in the evenings.

It's our privilege to enjoy the breezes blowing through the trees, to feel the warmth of the sun on our skin, and to hear the rain splashing to the Earth. Summer, fall, winter, and spring—we all get to relish the amazing seasons that God has created. To stroll through the woods or walk about the ocean shore is to enjoy God's goodness.

Each time God sends rain to water our flowers or gardens, we can savor His goodness. As trees grow and offer shade, we are also reminded of His kindness to us.

This is the handiwork of Almighty God. Therefore, a person has no excuse whatsoever for not believing in God. God's Word says it clearly and crisply. Romans 1:19-20 says, "Because what may be known of God is manifest in them, for God has shown it to them. For since the creation of the world His invisible attributes are clearly seen, being understood by the things that are made, even His eternal power and Godhead, so that they are without excuse."

APPLICATION

What about you? How have you experienced the goodness of God through His creation?

....

....

....

....

....

Which is your favorite season of the year? What do you love about it?

....

....

....

....

Take a minute and write out a prayer to God, thanking Him for His goodness in your life.

....

....

....

....

....

....

....

As I read today, teach me more about the importance of rest.

4

> But the seventh day is the Sabbath of the LORD your God.
> In it you shall do no work: you, nor your son, nor your daughter,
> nor your male servant, nor your female servant, nor your
> cattle, nor your stranger who is within your gates..
>
> **EXODUS 20:10**

The Chinese have a legend. They tell of the man who went to the marketplace one day and he had a string of seven coins. He saw a beggar and he gave the beggar six of those coins and placed the seventh in his pocket, but the beggar, who was also a pickpocket, lifted the seventh coin and took that for himself also. I'm afraid that's a parable of our modern day.

Our Lord has given us six days to do our work. But so many people take the six days and steal the seventh to use for themselves. Today's Scripture reminds us that there is one day a week when we are to honor the Lord with our time. We are to spend our six days working, and then give Him the seventh.

In the Old Testament, the Jewish Sabbath is the seventh day. Notice the verse, "But the seventh day is the Sabbath of the LORD your God." As New Testament Christians we do not worship on the seventh day, we worship on the first day. The seventh day is Saturday; the first day is Sunday. The seventh day is given to the Jew and is from the Old Testament. The first day is the Lord's Day and is given to the Christian from the New Testament.

The Early Church met for worship upon the first day of the week. We discover this in Acts 20:6-7. Collections were taken and received for the work of the Lord and the comfort of the saints upon the first day of the week. In 1 Corinthians 16:2, we read these instructions, "On the first day of the week let each one of you lay something aside, storing up as he may prosper, that there be no collections when I come."

APPLICATION

In your opinion, why does it matter that Christians meet on the first day of the week to worship together? Are you involved regularly with a community of believers?

....

....

....

....

....

Why do you think that resting one day a week is so important? Have you been able to rest one day per week?

....

....

....

....

....

Write out a prayer to the Lord in response to what you have read today.

....

....

....

....

....

....

Lord, show me the importance of Sunday rest and Sunday worship.

5

> And God spoke all these words, saying: "I am the LORD your God, who brought you out of the land of Egypt, out of the house of bondage. You shall have no other gods before Me."
>
> **EXODUS 20:1-3**

Why has our Lord ordained that we should worship? It is because of the nature of Man. Man is a spiritual being, and there are reasons for a day of rest in worship. First, worship gives you the chance to replenish your spirit. You can run down spiritually just like a battery can run down. God has given us a day to recharge, to replenish, to renew our spirits. Worship is meant to recharge our batteries.

A man in Philadelphia was passing a coal mine in the days when they used mules to pull the coal wagons through the mines. He noticed that one man had his mules in the pasture every Sunday. When asked why the mules were put out in the pastures on Sundays, the mule owner explained that the mules would go blind if they stayed in the coal mines all the time. They needed sunlight. To have one day a week grazing in the sunlight restored their vision and kept them working longer.

Similarly, some people work and live without ever taking a day off to rest and worship. We need to refresh our spirits, to reinvigorate our spirits, and to replenish our spirits. Also, God has given us a special day of worship that we might refresh our souls. Without this refreshing we become nervous, unstrung, anxious, taut, and tense.

Americans consume millions of pills to deal with anxiety and chaos. Our world is noisy and busy. And, we have invented so many new things. In reality, we have just added more noise and more speed. God says we had better slow down. We had better refresh our souls. Sundays give us a day to gain perspective, refocus, and refresh. Weekly worship assists with all of these endeavors.

APPLICATION

So, what does your typical Sunday look like? How do you like to spend your day?

....

....

....

....

Is worship a regular part of your Sunday schedule? If so, how has worship refreshed your soul and replenished your spirit?

....

....

....

....

Take a few moments to talk to the Lord about Sundays and worship. Use the space below to write out your prayer.

....

....

....

....

....

....

Open my heart and mind to discover more about the Biblical significance of rest.

6

> But those who wait on the LORD shall renew their strength;
> they shall mount up with wings like eagles, they shall
> run and not be weary, they shall walk and not faint.
>
> **ISAIAH 40:31**

A group of American explorers traveled to Africa. Once there, they hired some native guides to take them into the jungle. As soon as they hired the guides, their guides plunged quickly into the bush country to explore. They did this the first day, the second day, the third, the fourth, the fifth, and on the sixth day.

However, when they came to the seventh day, the guides refused to move. They sat down under a tree and would not budge. When the explorers tried to move them on, this is what they said. "We no go today; we rest today to let our souls catch up with our bodies."

Have you done that? Have you learned to be still and know that God is God? Have you learned in this neurotic, insane age how to deal with fears and worries and nervous tensions by refreshing the soul? God—who made us—knows how we are to operate.

We are to replenish our spirits, we are to refresh our souls, and then we are to rest our bodies. That's one of the main reasons that we worship. Worship is rest.

After six days of work, we need to rest our bodies for the preservation of health and renewal of strength. "But those who wait on the LORD shall renew their strength." Truly, there's something about coming to church and meeting with God's people that invigorates and renews you, if you worship right. Worship is meant to provide rest and restoration for a believer.

APPLICATION

What did you think about the story of the African guides? Do you find that your soul needs to catch up with your body too?

....

....

....

....

....

Have you also learned to be still and know that God is the Lord? What are some of the ways that you rest and refresh? What are some specific steps you can take to increase rest and refreshment?

....

....

....

....

....

Take a few moments to pray for wisdom to rest and renew your heart and life. Write out your prayer.

....

....

....

....

....

....

....

Lord, encourage me as I face my feelings of insecurity and inadequacy today.

7

> For you see your calling, brethren, that not many wise according to the flesh, not many mighty, not many noble, are called. But God has chosen the foolish things of the world to put to shame the wise, and God has chosen the weak things of the world to put to shame the things which are mighty; and the base things of the world and the things which are despised God has chosen, and the things which are not, to bring to nothing the things that are, that no flesh should glory in His presence.
>
> **1 CORINTHIANS 1:26-29**

nsecurity can impact all people at times. There are days where we can feel on top of the world—accomplished, capable, and realizing amazing feats. And, then there are other days. Maybe you have had to battle some recent feelings of inferiority or inadequacy?

Let's consider a few things that might lead to those feelings of insecurity. First, it may be that we don't feel like we measure up. If only we had that college degree, or a master's, or a doctorate. Besides, we can feel inferior by the clothes that we wear or the car that we drive. It may be that our feelings of inadequacy arise from a lack of money or prestige or title. Whatever the case, most of us will face moments during which we feel rather ordinary and unaccomplished.

In those moments, it is so good to remember something. The Bible tells us that God has a tremendous plan for our lives. God takes ordinary people and does extraordinary things through those ordinary people and gives glory to Himself.

We may not completely understand it, but the Bible reminds us, "God has chosen the foolish things of the world to put to shame the wise, and God has chosen the weak things of the world to put to shame the things which are mighty."

APPLICATION

Do you ever find yourself feeling insecure? What usually causes these feelings?

....

....

....

....

What do you think of this statement: God takes ordinary people and God does extraordinary things through those ordinary people and thereby God brings glory to Himself? How does this encourage you?

....

....

....

....

Finish your devotional time with prayer. Invite God to fill you with a greater sense of security and confidence in His plans for your life.

....

....

....

....

....

....

As I read today, I ask You to inspire me in Your calling for my life.

8

> For you see your calling, brethren, that not many wise according to the flesh, not many mighty, not many noble, are called. But God has chosen the foolish things of the world to put to shame the wise, and God has chosen the weak things of the world to put to shame the things which are mighty; and the base things of the world and the things which are despised God has chosen, and the things which are not, to bring to nothing the things that are, that no flesh should glory in His presence.
>
> **1 CORINTHIANS 1:26-29**

There was a man in the Bible whose name was Gideon. We find Gideon hiding on the threshing floor because the Midianites had invaded his land. Tucked away and afraid, Gideon was threshing wheat when an angel came to him.

When the angel appeared to him, he addressed Gideon as a mighty man of valor. If there's anything that Gideon was not, it was a mighty man of valor. Gideon was a chicken with a capital "C." He was afraid, he was in fear, and he was hiding out. However, the angel of the Lord called him a mighty man of valor. Further, the angel told Gideon that he would be a great deliverer of his people over the Midianites. However, Gideon reminded the angel that he was poor and from a modest home. His tribe was also poor and lowly and Gideon was the least in his father's house. Of all the tribes in Israel, Manasseh was the worst. Of all the families in Manasseh, Gideon's was the poorest. Of all the kids in the family, Gideon was the smallest.

Gideon felt like he was at the bottom of the barrel. How could God use him? Yet, God did use him; He used him in a mighty way. With just 300 men, Gideon led the Israelites to defeat the Midianites. God can do the same with you. You may feel like you are the least of the least or the lowest of the low, but our Lord specializes in getting great glory while using regular people. He does it all the time.

APPLICATION

Do you ever feel like you are insignificant in your work, home, or life? Why do you feel this way?

....

....

....

....

....

How does Gideon's story encourage you? What is one part of his story that gives you hope?

....

....

....

....

....

Take a few moments to write out a prayer to the Lord. Share your heart with Him today.

....

....

....

....

....

....

Open my heart to be more readily available to serve You.

9

> For you see your calling, brethren, that not many wise according to the flesh, not many mighty, not many noble, are called. But God has chosen the foolish things of the world to put to shame the wise, and God has chosen the weak things of the world to put to shame the things which are mighty; and the base things of the world and the things which are despised God has chosen, and the things which are not, to bring to nothing the things that are, that no flesh should glory in His presence.
>
> **1 CORINTHIANS 1:26-29**

Why does God use regular people to accomplish great things? Why does He use the weak to shame the strong and the foolish to shame the wise? In 1 Corinthians 1:29, we discover the reason, "that no flesh should glory in His presence."

In other words, there are not going to be any prancing proud "peacocks" in Heaven. There will be no superstars in Heaven. Why does God use ordinary people and give them extraordinary power? That no flesh should glory in His presence! All of the glory is to go to God, not to us.

What is the highest place in the world? It is not being Billy Graham, nor being the pastor of a megachurch. It is not writing a bestselling book, nor having a huge following on YouTube, Twitter, or Instagram. The highest place in the world is the center of the will of God for you, wherever that is.

If you want to be used by God, you can be used by God. He may choose a different way to use your life than you would have chosen. But if you will make yourself available to God, He will put you to work. You don't choose your place of service. If you make yourself available to Him, you will find your greatest ability is availability.

Many days, my prayer is simply this, "Lord Jesus, inhabit my humanity and do what You want to do in me."

APPLICATION

Why do you suppose God set up His economy of greatness as He did? Does it seem backward to you?

How have you seen God use you when you made yourself available? Note the experience below.

As you pray today, why not pray this prayer: "Lord Jesus, inhabit my humanity and do what you want to do in me."

Lord, I ask You to reignite my love and passion for worshiping You.

> "A son honors his father, and a servant his master. If then I am the Father, where is My honor? And if I am a Master, where is My reverence?" says the LORD of hosts to you priests who despise My name. Yet you say, "In what way have we despised Your name?"
>
> **MALACHI 1:6**

What do you do when you are weary of, and in, worship? Perhaps the greatest malady of our age is not lack of worship, but lack of true worship. So many people trudge to church Sunday after Sunday like they are doing God some wild favor for just being there. As they sit in church, they check things off on the Sunday bulletin, look at what is happening around them, and eagerly wait for church to be over.

It is as if we are doing our Sunday duty again. Weariness begins to set in. The thrill is gone. The excitement is gone, and we serve the Lord without any zeal, fervor, or joy. If you are in that place today, you are in a dangerous predicament. When worship becomes ho-hum and bland, we need to wake up.

The story is told of one man who had missed church for a while. As he was out running errands one day, he bumped into his pastor in the store. They exchanged pleasantries, and then the pastor mentioned how much they had missed the man and his family in church. Excuses gushed forth... sick kids, job requirements, traveling, ball games, family commitments, and even bad weather were offered as explanations.

Perhaps you can relate. It's so easy to miss a week and then another. It's also easy to show up week after week without any passion or excitement about worship. Perhaps that's what Malachi is addressing in verse 6, "If then I am the Father, where is My honor? And if I am a Master, where is My reverence?"

APPLICATION

What is worship like for you right now? On a scale of 1-10 (with 10 being greatest), where would you rate your worship?

_____

_____

_____

_____

_____

If church attendance has become boring, or even nonexistent for you, what has led you to this place in your life? Why do you think you've lost interest?

_____

_____

_____

_____

_____

Take a few moments to honestly pray about your feelings about church and worship. Write out your prayer in the space below.

_____

_____

_____

_____

_____

_____

_____

As I study today, show me any areas of my life that have become lukewarm.

11

> "A son honors his father, and a servant his master. If then I am the Father, where is My honor? And if I am a Master, where is My reverence?" says the LORD of hosts to you priests who despise My name. Yet you say, "In what way have we despised Your name?"
>
> **MALACHI 1:6**

Do we recognize the nature of God? As you read the verse today, you will discover that sons are to honor their fathers and servants are to honor their masters. It's the way it works best. Similarly, God says that He is both a father and a master. That's His nature. And He is to be honored as both a father and a master in our lives.

What does the word "honor" mean? In the Hebrew language, the word "honor" signifies something to which we attach weight, seriousness and significance. If you don't take God seriously, worship is going to be a bother and an inconvenience for you. But when you understand that God is your Father, that you've been born into a family by a new birth, and how much He loves you, things will change. You won't approach God with boring or lackluster worship. Instead, you're going to come before the Lord with love and devotion to honor our great God.

Our Lord had rather you not come to church at all than to come to church and not take God seriously. Revelation 3:15-16 says, "I know your works, that you are neither cold nor hot. I could wish you were cold or hot. So then, because you are lukewarm, and neither cold nor hot, I will vomit you out of My mouth."

God had rather have you cold—out and out against Him—than to have you lukewarm, coming to church, insulting Him with half-hearted worship. G. Campbell Morgan said that half-hearted worship or lukewarmness is the worst form of blasphemy. It is worse than not even believing in God. Why? Because lukewarmness says to God that you believe in Him but aren't really interested in worshiping Him. To be lukewarm is to be bored by your relationship with Almighty God.

APPLICATION

So, what is your spiritual temperature today? Are you hot, cold, or lukewarm? Why?

....

....

....

....

Why do you suppose God hates our lukewarmness and spiritual boredom so much? What can we do to show more honor for the Lord?

....

....

....

....

Pray today and invite God to reignite the passion in your heart for knowing Him. Invite Him to give you a greater love for Him and His Word. You may want to write out your prayer.

....

....

....

....

....

Lord, speak to my heart about revering You more.

12

> "A son honors his father, and a servant his master. If then I am the Father, where is My honor? And if I am a Master, where is My reverence?" says the LORD of hosts to you priests who despise My name. Yet you say, "In what way have we despised Your name?"
>
> **MALACHI 1:6**

What is reverence? It's sometimes referred to as having a fear of God. Does that mean that we quake in our boots as we think of God? No. It means that we come before His presence with holy awe, a reverence. In today's verse, the idea of our being servants is the idea of being bondslaves.

A bondslave is someone who's been bought out of the marketplace of sin and put into the service of our Lord and Savior Jesus Christ. 1 Corinthians 6:19 puts it this way, "Or do you not know that your body is the temple of the Holy Spirit who is in you, whom you have from God, and you are not your own?"

We are bought with a price; therefore, we're to glorify God in our bodies and in our spirits. As we enter into worship, we are to come with attitudes of honor and respect. For the fear (honor) of the Lord is the beginning of wisdom. The fear of the Lord is clean, right, and good.

Exodus 20:3 reminds us, "You shall have no other gods before Me." Often, however, we sit in the church filled with indifference. Other things, people, situations, decisions, and thoughts fill our minds. Although our bodies are in worship, our hearts are not.

When we attend church, participate in worship, or join a community of believers, it's the chance to also spend time with God the Father. As we enter worship, we may want to start with a simple prayer. We might pray something like this: God, in everything I do, I want to honor You. As I sit, talk, smile, sing, listen, interact, and pray, I want to honor You. You are my Father. I'm your child. You are my Master. I'm Your servant. My great desire is to bring You honor today. I want to show you incredible reverence in all that I do.

APPLICATION

What is your church, community, place of worship like? Describe it below.

_____

_____

_____

_____

On a scale of 1–10 (with 10 being greatest), how would you rate your worship right now? What changes would you like to make?

_____

_____

_____

_____

Why not take a few minutes to pray about worship? You can write out a prayer in the space below.

_____

_____

_____

_____

_____

_____

Father, teach me more of what it means to fear You.

13

> "A son honors his father, and a servant his master. If then I am the Father, where is My honor? And if I am a Master, where is My reverence?" says the LORD of hosts to you priests who despise My name. Yet you say, "In what way have we despised Your name?"
>
> **MALACHI 1:6**

Fear of the Lord. What is the fear of the Lord? It's not cringing dread of God. It is the reverence that is due His name—the worship, the praise, the awe of the awesome, mighty God who is our Master. I'll tell you what the fear of the Lord is. It is love on its knees. And the one who fears God the most loves Him the best.

We learn to fear and love God more by understanding His nature. Malachi explains that we are to respect—and not despise—the nature of God. If you would put excitement into your worship, you need to learn to reverence the name of God. "'Where is My reverence?' says the LORD of hosts to you priests who despise My name."

What had made the priests weary in worship? Why were they lacking reverence for God? They had become flippant and had lost their awe of God. In the daily grind of life, they had become complacent in their love for the Lord. According to 1 Peter 2:9, we are also priests of the Lord. The verse puts it this way, "But you are a chosen generation, a royal priesthood, a holy nation, His own special people, that you may proclaim the praises of Him who called you out of darkness into His marvelous light."

We too can become priests who have lost our reverence for the Lord and have despised His name. It's so easy to attend church, sing without passion, listen without paying attention, and worship with dry eyes and cold hearts. Without even realizing it, we quit taking God seriously. If this is the case in your life, why not invite God to renew your love and your reverence for Him today?

APPLICATION

What did you think of this definition of the fear of the Lord as "love on its knees"?

....

....

....

....

Over the last weeks and months, have you stopped taking God seriously? If so, why do you think this has happened?

....

....

....

....

Take a few moments to pray and invite God to reignite your love and reverence for Him. Use the space below to journal your prayer.

....

....

....

....

....

....

....

Lord, bless these moments I'm about to spend in Your Word today.

14

> Then David said to the Philistine, "You come to me with a sword, with a spear, and with a javelin. But I come to you in the name of the LORD of hosts, the God of the armies of Israel, whom you have defied."
>
> **1 SAMUEL 17:45**

David won the victory by three principles. First of all, there is a principle of purpose. David said, "I will." Despite the disdain of others, despite the derision of others, and despite the discouragement of others, David stepped up and fought the giant. David was full of purpose. Nothing that others did or said pushed him off course.

Also, in this story, there is a principle of progression. He said to that Philistine, "I slew a lion and a bear, and I'll get you, too." David was faithful in that which was least, so he was able to be faithful in that which was much. First, he took care of his sheep and protected them from lions and bears. Then, he protected his fellow Israelites from Goliath. Truly, he went from victory unto victory.

Also, there was the principle of power. David knew that the battle was the Lord's. And he said, "You come to me with a sword, with a spear, and with a javelin. But I come to you in the name of the LORD of hosts." David knew the power that was his. Therefore, he won the victory in the strength of the Lord.

Victory can be ours today as well. As we purpose to do what God has called us to do, progress as God leads, and depend upon His power, you and I can experience great things.

APPLICATION

How does the story of David and Goliath encourage you? What is your favorite part of the story?

....

....

....

....

In your own life, where do you need a victory today? What is your greatest struggle right now?

....

....

....

....

Conclude your devotional time by praying about your biggest struggle today. Invite God to intervene and to work a miracle.

....

....

....

....

....

....

Lord, teach me about the absolute power that is in the name of Jesus.

15

> "For from the rising of the sun, even to its going down, My name shall be great among the Gentiles; in every place incense shall be offered to My name, and a pure offering; for My name shall be great among the nations," says the Lord of hosts.
>
> **MALACHI 1:11**

God's name needs to be declared. Look again at today's verse. "For from the rising of the sun, even to its going down, My name shall be great among the Gentiles; in every place incense shall be offered to My name." What is this verse talking about? It's talking about the time when Jesus would come and live on the Earth. Indeed, Malachi looked forward to the time when Jesus—the Son of God—would come and minister to the Gentiles.

Do you know what the name "Jesus" means? It means Jehovah saves. The name of Jesus is like sweet incense all over the world. As people praise His name, the incense rises to the Father. Moreover, we are people of the name of Jesus. We are saved by the name of Jesus. In Acts 4:12, we are reminded, "Nor is there salvation in any other, for there is no other name under heaven given among men by which we must be saved."

When you and I worship, we worship in the name of Jesus. There is great authority in the name of Jesus. In Matthew 18:20, Jesus said to His disciples, "For where two or three are gathered together in My name, I am there in the midst of them."

In the name of Jesus, we find hope, encouragement, answered prayer, comfort, and help. As we worship in His name, we experience Him more and learn to trust Him more.

There is power in the name of Jesus. And, when you and I worship in His name, our worship will begin to grow and to come alive. Vibrant worship happens when we lift up the name of Jesus.

APPLICATION

Have you ever thought about the significance of worshiping in Jesus' name? Why does this matter?

_____

_____

_____

_____

_____

How would you rate the vibrancy of your worship right now? Is it alive and powerful? If not, why not?

_____

_____

_____

_____

_____

Pray in the name of Jesus today. Lift Him up. Praise Him. Tell Jesus how much you love Him.

_____

_____

_____

_____

_____

_____

_____

Lord, show me more about what it means to be a friend of Jesus.

16

> "For from the rising of the sun, even to its going down, My name shall be great among the Gentiles; in every place incense shall be offered to My name, and a pure offering; for My name shall be great among the nations," says the LORD of hosts.
>
> **MALACHI 1:11**

Pastor Ron Dunn tells a wonderful story of a time when his kids were small. His entire extended family was at a county fair having the time of their lives. Children, cousins, and all sorts of family members had joined the festivities. To make things run smoother, Brother Ron purchased a huge roll of carnival tickets to share with the whole family.

Knowing how much his family loved to ride the rides, Ron wanted to make sure he had plenty of tickets for the entire day. The children would line up and tell him what ride was next. Then, he'd pull off a few tickets and hand them to the kids. After each Ferris wheel ride, octopus ride, and mini car ride, the children would come back to him with their hands raised—ready for the next ride. All day long, Pastor Ron would stand in front of each ride, tear off tickets, and watch the children having the time of their lives.

At one point, a very strange thing happened. A little boy that Ron had never seen came up to him and put out his hand. Unsure of what to do next, Ron paused for a minute. But then his son came up to him and told him that the stranger was his friend, Jimmy. Ron's son had promised Jimmy that his daddy would give him some tickets. To honor his son's words, Brother Ron gave Jimmy the tickets. Little Jimmy was able to enjoy free rides at the fair that day because of Ron's son.

This is why we pray in the name of Jesus. Because God loves and honors His Son, we reap the benefits when we pray. Since we are the friends of Jesus, we get to enjoy the sweet "rides" of the Christian life. From the rising of the sun to the going down of the same, the Lord's name is to be praised. Indeed, there's salvation, authority, security, joy, and hope in the name of Jesus.

APPLICATION

Have you ever been to a carnival or a county fair that required tickets to ride? What was your favorite ride?

....

....

....

....

You are a friend of Jesus with access to God. Friendship with Jesus brings salvation, authority, security, joy, and hope. How does this encourage you today?

....

....

....

....

Why not take a few minutes to pray and honor the name of Jesus? You can write out your prayer below.

....

....

....

....

....

....

Lord, show me how I can freely enjoy living in the presence of Almighty God.

17

Perhaps one day, you or I have the President of the United States visit our town, church, or community. It is possible.

In one church, the President had been talking with the leadership about a possible visit. Word got out in the community that the President might come. Many people who did not normally attend decided they wanted to be there that particular Sunday.

One woman in the community was especially impressed and called the church to find out more. When asked about whether or not the President might be attending the services that week, she was told that he would not be able to make it. However, the woman was informed by the staff, "the President will not be here Sunday, but the King of kings will be."

When we attend church, we are in the highest company possible. There is no greater audience than the King of kings and Lord of lords. Perhaps, it would be special to have one of the Presidents or a celebrity in our midst. We would all want pictures and want all of our friends to know what had happened. It would be fun to post a selfie with someone famous.

However, Jesus is with us always. He promises never to leave us or forsake us. When we are in our homes, workplaces, at the gym, and in church, He is there too. Every day, we get to enjoy His presence and we have an immediate audience with Almighty God. In Psalm 16:11, we read, "You will show me the path of life; in Your presence is fullness of joy; at Your right hand are pleasures forevermore."

APPLICATION

Who is the most famous person you have ever met or been in the room with? What was it like?

....

....

....

....

How does it make you feel to know that you can freely enjoy living in the presence of Almighty God? What difference has this made in your life?

....

....

....

....

For a few minutes, enjoy time in His presence. Be still. Look up. Tell Jesus how much you love and appreciate Him.

....

....

....

....

....

Lord, teach me today about Your transforming love.

> ...when He comes, in that Day, to be glorified in His saints and to be admired among all those who believe, because our testimony among you was believed.
>
> **2 THESSALONIANS 1:10**

There is a day when something amazing is going to happen. Jesus is going to return to this Earth. Second Thessalonians 1:10 tells us, "...when He comes, in that Day, to be glorified in His saints and to be admired."

The word "admired" carries the idea of wonder and awe. J.B. Phillips translates it this way, "It will be a breathtaking wonder to all that believe."

Can you imagine what it would be like if we heard the trumpets sound right now and we were swept up in the clouds to be with Him? It would be an awesome thing! And it would likely cause us to wonder at Him. Do you know what we'll wonder at?

We will wonder at His transforming and redeeming love. God has taken stubborn, ignorant, blind, and difficult people, and transformed them by His love. His love has opened blind eyes. Those who'd been demonized by the power of lust and drugs and immorality have been made pure. What transforming love this is!

At this moment, we will be caught up to meet the Lord and changed. In a moment, in the twinkling of an eye, we'll look around and see the saints in their glorified bodies. The Bible tells us we will be like Him—exalted as prophets, priests, and kings. We will reign with Him, and every vestige of sin will be removed. It will be wonderful, and it will fill us all with wonder.

For years, George Beverly Shea used to sing this song at the Billy Graham Crusades, "O, the wonder of it all! The wonder of it all! Just to think that God loves me. O, the wonder of it all! The wonder of it all! Just to think that God loves me."

APPLICATION

When is the last time that you were blown away by something or by someone? What happened?

....

....

....

....

As you think about Jesus coming again, and about His transforming love, what comes to mind? How has God's love transformed your life?

....

....

....

....

In the next few moments, thank God for transforming you. Thank Him for His love, power, and goodness to you.

....

....

....

....

....

Lord, speak to my heart as I read today about the gift of salvation.

19

> ...when He comes, in that Day, to be glorified in His
> saints and to be admired among all those who believe,
> because our testimony among you was believed.
>
> **2 THESSALONIANS 1:10**

When the Bible uses the word "all," it literally means all. In the verse above, we read the words, "all those who believe." God's saving grace is available to all people. His saving grace is wonderful and is freely offered to every man, woman, boy, and girl.

Also, notice that saving grace doesn't have any special parameters or conditions. The conditions are simple, "all those who believe." He doesn't say, "all those who did wonderful works." He doesn't say, "all of those who gave a lot of money." He doesn't say, "all of those who are beautiful or brilliant." No! We will wonder that we have been saved by His grace! We just put our faith where God put our sins, upon the Lord Jesus Christ.

Does that seem too simple to you? It is gloriously simple and it is simply glorious. "Believe on the Lord Jesus Christ, and you will be saved" (Acts 16:31). If you believe in Jesus, I promise you on the authority of the Word of God, He will save you. God can save anybody, anywhere, anytime, who comes to Jesus in repentance of faith. He will save you.

Additionally, we are promised that God is able to keep us. This is the wonder of His keeping power. In today's verse, we read, "He's coming to be glorified...among all those that believe." Not one of His children will be lost. All who believe will be saved and kept.

Truly, the same God that saves you is the God that will keep you securely in His grip. This truth is highlighted in John 10:28-29, "And I give them eternal life, and they shall never perish; neither shall anyone snatch them out of My hand. My Father, who has given them to Me, is greater than all; and no one is able to snatch them out of My Father's hand."

APPLICATION

How does it make you feel to know that Jesus came to save all people?

....

....

....

....

Have you received God's gift of salvation? If so, how has He changed your life? If not, why not receive Him today? All who call upon the name of the Lord will be saved.

....

....

....

....

As you pray today, ask God to give you an increased sense of security about your salvation. Invite Him to give you a rock-ribbed assurance that you are His.

....

....

....

....

....

....

Lord, show me what true family worship looks like.

20

> "You shall have no other gods before Me. You shall
> not make for yourself a carved image—any likeness of
> anything that is in heaven above, or that is in the earth
> beneath, or that is in the water under the earth."
>
> **EXODUS 20:3-4**

Our scriptures today are the first two of the 10 Commandments. The first commandment tells us who to worship, "No other gods." The second commandment tells us how to worship. The first commandment forbids false gods. And the second commandment forbids false worship.

How does this apply to us and to our families? The greatest gift you can give to your kids and grandkids is to teach them to worship. You couldn't teach them anything any more important than that. And yet, how many children today learn to worship in the home?

Some people feel like taking their children to church, youth group, Bible study, and even Christian school will meet the need for worship. However, if our children do not see Jesus in our homes, then everything else may become a waste of time. Think about it. We attend church and act all godly, but then we bicker around the breakfast table. The worship that does not begin at home, does not begin at all.

The commandment tells us to not falsely worship. Now, this is set in the negative, but anything that is in the negative has to have a positive, or it could not be negative. So what is the positive in this passage?

The positive instruction for us today is to be people who truly worship and teach our families to truly worship. As we fall in love with Jesus and share His love, those closest to us will be impacted. Worship Him at home, and your children will take notice.

APPLICATION

Why do you think parents rely so heavily on churches, youth groups, and Christian schools to teach their children about God?

....

....

....

....

Do you feel that you are modeling true worship in your home and family? What are some ways you share Christ with your family at home?

....

....

....

....

As you pray today, talk these things over with the Lord. Allow Him to show you areas where you could add more worship to your days and to your family times. Jot down any ideas you receive as you pray.

....

....

....

....

....

....

As I study about You as the Master of my life, reveal any areas where I am holding back.

21

"You shall have no other gods before Me. You shall not make for yourself a carved image—any likeness of anything that is in heaven above, or that is in the earth beneath, or that is in the water under the earth."

EXODUS 20:3-4

Fritz Kreisler was one of the greatest violinists of all time. He had a Stradivarius violin. There are only a few Stradivarius violins in the entire world. Let me tell you how he got it. At one time, the violin that Fritz Kreisler played belonged to a wealthy Englishman. Fritz Kreisler learned about the violin and tried to buy it.

However, the Englishman told him that it was not for sale. Kreisler didn't give up. In time, he went to visit that Englishman and humbly asked to just touch the violin. He was granted his request. But rather than just touching the violin, Kreisler took a little advantage and he tucked it under his chin and began to draw the bow across those strings. When Fritz Kreisler began to play that violin, you could hear the laughter of children in the streets. You could hear birds singing. You could just hear the music of the spheres.

The old Englishman listened for a while and then great tears began to course down his cheeks. When Fritz Kreisler realized he'd pushed it a little far by taking that violin into his hands, he quickly apologized. He admitted that he shouldn't have played it, but he would love to own the violin. Unexpectedly, the wealthy Englishman said, "It's not for sale. But, you may have it. You are the master. It doesn't belong to me. It now belongs to you."

Likewise, God is the only one who is worthy of your life. Our lives belong to Him and no one else. He is the Master, and we are His. Truly, you must give your heart, your life, and all that you have to Him in worship. Just as the Englishman gave his violin to the master violinist, we must give our lives to the Master of the Universe.

APPLICATION

What did you think about the violin story? Could you relate? Are you a musician?

Answer this question as honestly as possible: Is God the Master of your life? Are there any areas where you are holding back?

Take a few minutes to pray and give everything to God today. You might even make a list of the five most important things or people in your life. Then, pray and give each of these to the Lord.

Lord, reveal any idols that I am worshiping more than You.

22

Their idols are silver and gold, the work of men's hands. They have mouths, but they do not speak; eyes they have, but they do not see; they have ears, but they do not hear; noses they have, but they do not smell; they have hands, but they do not handle; feet they have, but they do not walk; nor do they mutter through their throat. Those who make them are like them; so is everyone who trusts in them... O house of Aaron, trust in the LORD; He is their help and their shield.

PSALM 115:4-8, 10

One of the most essential ingredients in worship is to have a proper conception of God. If you conceive God wrongly, you're going to behave wrongly. The verses in today's devotional describe the stupidity, the silliness, of worshiping anything but Almighty God. In verse 8, the Psalmist says, "those who make them are like them."

What does this mean? As we make idols in our homes and lives, we begin to be molded into the shape and form of our idols. Think about it. We become like what we worship. If we worship sports, sports can become our idol. The same is true with money, power, popularity, work, or the pursuit of pleasure. The Bible teaches that we will become like those things that we most pursue.

So it is very important that we have a proper conception of God. Not just any god. We must understand who God is and what God is like. Therefore, God has absolutely forbidden the making of anything material as an object of worship. Why? Because God is not a material God; He is spiritual.

The Bible tells us in John 4:24 that "God is Spirit, and those who worship Him must worship in spirit and truth." It says that God is Spirit, not a spirit. He is Spirit. That is His essence. God is Spirit and to worship Him, we must worship Him in spirit and truth. Also, He is the only person, place, or thing that we are to worship. No one else and nothing else should be the object of our worship.

APPLICATION

Have you ever thought about idols? In your experience, what are some of the idols people worship?

....

....

....

....

....

Is there an "idol" you are tempted to worship? Is there anything or any person that competes for your worship?

....

....

....

....

....

As you pray today, ask God to move you to the place where He is the supreme object of your worship. Talk these things over with Him.

....

....

....

....

....

....

Lord, cleanse my heart and open it to Your message for me today.

23

> "To whom then will you liken Me, or to whom shall I be equal?" says the Holy One.
>
> **ISAIAH 40:25**

What would you say God is most like? To whom would you compare God? Who is His equal?

You'll make a big mistake if you'll say God is compared to anything. What are you going to say God is like? You can say one man is like another man. One piano is like another piano. One pulpit is like another pulpit. One suit is like another suit. However, there is only one God.

There's nothing else to compare God to. In the first place, He is spiritual and the material can never represent the spiritual. Secondly, He is in a class and a category all by Himself. Any idol is a bad picture of God. And who wants a bad picture of himself or herself in circulation? Think about it. When we come across bad pictures, we just discard them. We don't like pictures that make us look bad. Conversely, if there are photos that make us look good, we share them.

The Bible speaks of people who have changed the glory of the incorruptible God into an image made like a corruptible man. And we all have a desire to worship something. Truly, nature abhors a vacuum. Man is incurably religious and if he doesn't worship the true God in the right way, he's going to worship something else.

Do you know what an idol is? An idol is a magnified sinner. What a man does is to take his worst vices and make gods out of them. Then he worships those vices and legitimizes them. For some people, success can become the idol that they worship. For others, it may be popularity or travel or clothes or food. Anything can become an idol.

Any vice can become something we worship. That's the reason that idolatry is such a horrible thing. Idolatry causes us to transfer our greatest affections and our adoration from Almighty God to some other person, place, or thing. Only God is to be our source!

APPLICATION

Have you ever had a picture taken of you that you loved? Hated? What did you do with the one that you loved? What about the one you hated?

....

....

....

....

....

What did you think of this definition of an idol: An idol is a magnified sinner? Do you agree? How have you seen this to be true in your own experiences?

....

....

....

....

....

Ask God to reveal any idols you have set up in your own life. Give Him those idols and commit to make God your only source again today.

....

....

....

....

....

....

....

As I study today, show me any ways that I have become the center of my universe.

24

> You shall not bow down to them nor serve them. For I, the LORD your God, am a jealous God, visiting the iniquity of the fathers upon the children to the third and fourth generations of those who hate Me.
>
> **EXODUS 20:5**

What does the Bible mean when it says that God is a jealous God? In this text, we read, "I, the LORD your God, am a jealous God." To understand this concept, we must know that there are two kinds of jealousy. In the wrong sense, there can be a terrible form of jealousy. It's the type of jealousy that we refer to as the green-eyed monster. When others are thinner than us, smarter than us, sing better than we do, or make more money than we do, we can get jealous. And not in a good way.

However, this is not the jealousy referenced as God's jealousy. Instead, there is a holy jealousy, righteous jealousy. God has every right to be jealous of Who He is because there's only one God. Only one, not two. He has a monopoly on being God. He has holy jealousy and He is a jealous God.

What is He jealous over? Most of us don't make wooden idols, but we do worship other things. The Bible talks about the idolatry of the heart. Ezekiel 14:3a expresses it this way, "these men have set up their idols in their hearts."

What are some of these idols of the heart? One of the idols we set up today is to make idols of ourselves. We can make big deals out of us! We've gone from theology to me-ology. Have you noticed that? Instead of worshiping the Creator, we are adoring the creation. In 2 Timothy 3:2a, we are told that in the last days people will be "lovers of themselves."

Anything that we love more, fear more, or serve more than God, is an idol. If we love ourselves and serve ourselves more than we love and serve God, it's possible that we may have begun making our wishes and our desires an idol. We have become the god that we worship.

APPLICATION

Have you ever thought about the jealousy of God? How is His jealousy different from ours?

....

....

....

....

....

Are there any ways in which you have made yourself the center of your universe? It's so easy to do. Why not take a few minutes and invite God to show you areas that need to be given back to Him?

....

....

....

....

....

Take a few minutes and offer adoration to the Lord today. Worshiping God is one of the fastest ways to take the focus off ourselves and place it back on Him.

....

....

....

....

....

....

....

Lord, bless these moments that I am about to spend with You in Your Word today.

25

> You shall not bow down to them nor serve them. For I, the LORD your God, am a jealous God, visiting the iniquity of the fathers upon the children to the third and fourth generations of those who hate Me.
>
> **EXODUS 20:5**

s God the Lord of your life? If not, what things have you allowed to take over as the gods of your life? For example, some people have made a god out of money. They avoid church because churches just want to take all of their money. In honesty, their lives are ruled by greed. Their creed is, "Get all you can, can all you get, sit on the lid and poison the rest." To those who worship money, they serve at the place of the almighty dollar. However, Jesus said, "Ye cannot serve God and mammon" (Matthew 6:24b). You just can't do it. Either God is God or money is God.

Additionally, some worship their homes and their families. Really. Rather than being in church on Sundays, they are out doing family things. They are at sporting events, ballet recitals, with their families at the lake, or visiting family in another state. There is nothing wrong with loving our families, but when we put them before God, we are making a mistake. Jesus said, "He who loves father or mother more than Me is not worthy of Me" (Matthew 10:37a).

The best thing you can do for your family is to put them second. For example, my wife doesn't mind being in second place in my heart. She is in second place; God is in first place. Because I love God first, I can love my wife more and better. God gives me a love for her and a kindness in dealing with her that I would not have apart from Him. Deeply loving the Lord and making Him my priority causes me to be a better husband, father, and grandfather.

The same can be true in your life. As you make God your greatest priority, He will bless your home and your family. Don't make a god of your family. Our Lord warned against making a god of our families. Instead, make Him Lord, and all of your other relationships will benefit.

APPLICATION

Why do you think it's so easy to make an idol out of our marriages, children, families, and homes?

_____

_____

_____

_____

_____

In your own life, do you struggle with the idol of your family? If so, where do you struggle? If not, why not?

_____

_____

_____

_____

_____

Take a few moments to pray and invite God to make you a better and more understanding spouse, parent, grandparent, or family member. You may want to write out your prayer.

_____

_____

_____

_____

_____

_____

_____

Help me to agree with You, Lord, about the things that are in my heart today.

26

> Nevertheless even among the rulers many believed in Him, but because of the Pharisees they did not confess Him, lest they should be put out of the synagogue.
>
> **JOHN 12:42**

What are some of the things in our lives that we are tempted to worship instead of God?

For example, we can be tempted to worship the gods of popularity. Truly, I believe that there are some mothers today who would let their daughters spend a weekend in Hell if they thought it would make them more popular. Look again at today's verse.

What does this verse mean? It means that many people will believe in Jesus but not make their faith in Him public. They fear that public association with Jesus Christ will negatively impact their other associations. To be well thought of by others, they will not confess Christ in public, in their communities, or at their jobs. So, they keep their relationship with Jesus private and personal.

Additionally, many who are concerned with the god of popularity will not make a public decision for Christ. They want to walk a church aisle and take a stand for Christ. Further, they would love to be baptized. But what would people think? What might others say? Their god is the opinion of other people. They love and fear the opinion of other people more than they love and fear God. At times, people-pleasing is a temptation for all of us.

The Apostle Paul shared the challenge in this way in Galatians 1:10, "...Or do I seek to please men? For if I still pleased men, I would not be a bondservant of Christ."

APPLICATION

Do you ever find yourself tempted to worship the god of popularity? Why do you suppose it has such a strong pull on most people?

....

....

....

....

What are some ways you have found to fight the temptation to please others? How are you seeking to please God?

....

....

....

....

The struggle is real. Pray today and talk over this issue of popularity and people-pleasing with the Lord.

....

....

....

....

....

....

Lord, teach me today how to better model family worship for my family.

27

A woman approached her pastor to talk to him about the spiritual training of her child. She asked what age she should begin to teach her child about God. Five years old? Three years old? Three months old? The pastor unexpectedly told her that none of those ages was early enough. Instead, he suggested that spiritual training should begin with the grandparents and parents and be passed along to the children. Faith is to be passed down from generation to generation.

As parents, it's not enough for you to have theological exactitude. It's not enough for you to attend church and take notes. It's not enough to go to Bible studies, read Christian books, and listen to inspirational music. "God is Spirit, and those who worship Him must worship in spirit and truth" (John 4:24).

But how does that play out in your family? How are you teaching your children about the worship of God? It is the greatest thing you can do for your children. God deserves it. The word *worship* comes from *worth-ship*. God desires it, the Father seeketh such. God demands it. "You shall worship the LORD your God, and Him only."

As parents and grandparents, you and I must consider some challenging questions. Do you worship the one true God? Do you worship Him in spirit and in truth? Do your children know that you love Him more than anything else? Do your grandchildren, nieces and nephews, and other younger relatives know this? The best thing you can do for your children is to teach them to worship God.

My children and grandchildren know that I am not perfect. But I'll tell you something else they know. All of them will tell you that they know I'm not a phony. They know I love God and put Him at the forefront of my life.

APPLICATION

Are you a parent? Grandparent? Uncle or aunt? Who are you able to mentor and teach?

....

....

....

....

....

In what ways have you modeled worship for your family? What are some ways you would like to model worship in the coming days?

....

....

....

....

....

Pray and invite God to use you to impact the generations who will come after you.

....

....

....

....

....

....

....

As I study, I ask You to teach me more about what it is to truly worship.

28

Do you know your greatest need? Maybe you think it's a need for more money, for a husband or wife, for a new car, or to lose 20 pounds? But, as important as those things may seem, they are not your greatest need. Your greatest need is to learn to worship God. To worship in spirit and in truth is the ultimate privilege. And to worship God is, beyond a doubt, the supreme duty of any child of God. Let me repeat it for emphasis. *To worship is your greatest need.* To worship is your ultimate privilege. To worship is your supreme duty.

We are invited, we are commanded, we are encouraged, we are empowered, to worship Him. That is the bottom line. Going to Heaven is not the bottom line. We go to Heaven to worship Him. Being saved is not the bottom line. We're saved so that we can worship Him. And your life would be better if you worshiped better.

Why worship? Very simply this...we become like what we worship. Whatever a person worships conforms to that person. According to Psalm 115:8, "Those who make them are like them; so is everyone who trusts in them." In other words, when we form idols, idols begin to mold us. We become like what we worship. If we learn to worship God, He transforms us and molds us to be like Him.

When you put a poker in the fire and leave it in there long enough, the fire is in the poker. It comes out glowing and red hot. When you immerse yourself in the presence of God, the presence of God begins to get in you. True worship will make you more like the One you worship.

APPLICATION

What are some of your greatest tangible needs right now? Relationship needs? Job needs? Financial needs? Family needs?

....

....

....

....

....

Why do we worship the Lord? What difference does it make in our lives?

....

....

....

....

Take a few moments to pray and invite God to make you more like Him. Ask Him to grow your passion and desire to worship.

....

....

....

....

....

....

Lord, help me to apply these verses and insights to my life today.

29

> So He came to a city of Samaria which is called Sychar, near the plot of ground that Jacob gave to his son Joseph. Now Jacob's well was there. Jesus therefore, being wearied from His journey, sat thus by the well. It was about the sixth hour. A woman of Samaria came to draw water. Jesus said to her, "Give Me a drink."
>
> **JOHN 4:5-7**

Do you know what's wrong with the modern church today? We have forgotten how to truly worship the Lord.

Some will say that to build a great church you must talk about the needs of people. Help them to have their needs met, and they will love the church. Address their emotional, psychological, physical needs, and they will faithfully attend. Scratch them where they itch. However, this makes worship all about humans and not about God. Rather than worshiping God, we come and we turn our eyes inward upon ourselves seeking to find life.

Jesus taught, however, that to save our lives, we must give them up. In Matthew 16:25, He taught, "For whoever desires to save his life will lose it, but whoever loses his life for My sake will find it." If you want to be utterly miserable, turn your life inward. But, if you want to be filled with joy, turn your focus upward. Look into the face of God and learn to worship.

The verses in today's devotion are about a miserable woman. The reason she is unhappy is that she has never learned to worship. Self-centered, blinded by Satan, a slave to sin, she has found the things of the world to be unfulfilling. As she has moved from one husband to another, she has found no satisfaction. After five failed marriages, she is living with a man. She thought that she could find joy in these things, but it is all turned to dust and lost its allure.

In her sorrow, she comes face to face with Jesus. The conversation starts with religion but quickly moves to something more. At the well, on this particular day, this woman begins to learn about true worship. Her encounter with Jesus completely changes her life.

APPLICATION

Have you ever thought about what brings people to church? What are the main things that attract people to your church?

....

....

....

....

....

Why do you think worship is so important in our churches and in our lives? Why does it matter that we worship God?

....

....

....

....

....

Take a few moments and ask God to show you any ways that you have worshiped yourself more than Him. Ask Him to empower you to take your focus off yourself and place it on God alone.

....

....

....

....

....

....

As I study, reveal any unfulfilled longings in my heart and life.

30

> God, who made the world and everything in it, since He is Lord of heaven and earth, does not dwell in temples made with hands. Nor is He worshiped with men's hands, as though He needed anything, since He gives to all life, breath, and all things.
>
> **ACTS 17:24-25**

Why did God make you? Why were you created?

Some believe God made us to serve Him. Yet, if God wanted servants, He'd get angels not human beings. They're a lot more punctual and a lot more faithful. So, God didn't make you primarily to serve Him. Instead, He created you to worship Him, to love Him, to know Him, and to enjoy Him.

What did God make a fish to do? He made a fish to swim in the sea. What did God make a bird to do? He made a bird to fly in the air. What did God make you to do? God created you for Himself to enjoy Him and for Him to enjoy you. And until you do that, you'll never know fulfillment.

If you take a fish out of the sea and put him up in a tree, he's an unhappy fish. If you take a bird out of the air and put him under the water, he will be an unhappy bird. Similarly, if you take a man who is made for God and immerse him in the things of this world, he will be unhappy and unsatisfied. For apart from God, he will have no fulfillment.

That's what the Apostle Paul said in Acts 17:24-25 to the superstitious people on Mars Hill. Paul explained that they didn't even know what they were worshiping. God made us to worship Him, for in Him we live, and move, and have our being. The main element for a fish is the water. The main element for a bird is the air. And the main element for a child of God is God Himself. Until you learn to worship the Lord, you will be like a fish out of water. You'll be like a round peg in a square hole.

APPLICATION

Have you ever thought about why God made you? How would you answer this question: why did God create you?

....

....

....

....

Do you ever feel like a fish out of water? Like something is off or missing? Could this be related somehow to an unfulfilled longing in your heart for more of God?

....

....

....

....

Take a few moments to pray about these things today.

....

....

....

....

....

Lord, show me today as I read how I am wasting Your time and mine.

31

"You worship what you do not know; we know what we worship, for salvation is of the Jews. But the hour is coming, and now is, when the true worshipers will worship the Father in spirit and truth; for the Father is seeking such to worship Him. God is Spirit, and those who worship Him must worship in spirit and truth."

JOHN 4:22-24

What's the difference between true worship and false worship? And why does it matter?

We must learn the meaning of true worship as followers of Jesus Christ. In the story of the woman at the well, there is an interesting discussion all about worship. In the verses today, we read Jesus' response to this woman, "You worship what you do not know; we know what we worship..."

In Matthew 15:9a, Jesus said about the scribes and the Pharisees, "in vain do they worship." What is vain worship? What does it mean to worship in vain? One way people worship in vain is to worship some sort of idol. When you worship some New Age deity, some god of superstition, or some god of substance or success, or even yourself, this worship is in vain. Truly, many worship at the shrine of self. Then you provoke the Lord to jealousy because God says in Isaiah 42:8b, "My glory I will not give to another."

Vain worship could also include insincere worship. In Matthew 15:8, Jesus gave this solemn warning, "These people draw near to Me with their mouth, and honor Me with their lips, but their heart is far from Me."

Half-hearted worship is an insult to Almighty God. To sing and not mean what we sing is vain worship. To tell God that we will surrender all to Him, but then hold out a couple of personal things, this is vain worship. To pray without focus or read the Bible without concentrating, these are also a waste of our time and God's. The Lord wants us to worship whole-heartedly, completely, with great focus, with full attention, and with all of our might.

APPLICATION

Have you ever thought about the difference between true and false worship? What does it mean to worship in vain?

....

....

....

....

....

In your own life, how have you wasted God's time and yours? What two or three things can you do to practice more true worship regularly?

....

....

....

....

....

Take a few moments to pray. Invite God to move you away from any vain worship and toward more true worship.

....

....

....

....

....

....

....

Lord, speak to my heart as I read today and show me anything I need to make right.

— 32 —

> "Therefore if you bring your gift to the altar, and there remember that your brother has something against you, leave your gift there before the altar, and go your way. First be reconciled to your brother, and then come and offer your gift."
>
> **MATTHEW 5:23-24**

Have you ever been trying to pray, worship, or read the Bible and been reminded of something or someone? It's as if you get stuck in your worship because of this reminder. Perhaps you are at odds with a co-worker or neighbor or family member? Maybe you remember that you owe someone money. It could be you forgot to follow through on a promise or a pledge that you made to someone.

If you find a blockage as you are trying to worship God, this is likely sin in your life that God wants to deal with. When we worship God with sin in our hearts, God says in Isaiah 1:15, "When you spread out your hands, I will hide My eyes from you; even though you make many prayers, I will not hear. Your hands are full of blood." In other words, God will not hear our prayers when we have unconfessed sin in our lives. To worship God with an unclean heart is an abomination to God.

In Matthew 5, Jesus tells us that if you give money with hatred in your heart, or if you give money with unreconciled sins that are not made right, it is vain worship. It is an insult to Almighty God. God says, leave the money, go make it right with your brother. Go get right with your brother. Go get right with your sister. Go ask for forgiveness and then come and bring that offering.

To truly enjoy worship with God, we must be right with our fellow man and woman. Sin and unreconciled relationships clog up the prayer pipes. Reconciliation, forgiveness and restoration all open back up the sweet flow between God and us. Repairing things on the horizontal level also repairs things on the vertical level—bringing back the joy of worship again.

APPLICATION

Why do you suppose our relationships with other people have such an effect on our relationship with God?

....

....

....

....

Is there anything God wants you to make right today? Do you owe anyone money? Need to seek the forgiveness of another person? Need to return a library book or pay a fine?

....

....

....

....

As you pray today, invite God to turn His searchlight onto your life. Ask Him to show you anything you need to make right. If He points something out, make every effort to make amends.

....

....

....

....

....

Open my heart to desire more of You and to love You more.

> "You worship what you do not know; we know what we worship, for salvation is of the Jews. But the hour is coming, and now is, when the true worshipers will worship the Father in spirit and truth; for the Father is seeking such to worship Him. God is Spirit, and those who worship Him must worship in spirit and truth."
>
> **JOHN 4:22-24**

The story is told of a woman who was trapped in an apartment building. As she screamed for help, a brave fireman went up a ladder to rescue her. He took her in his arms and carried her down that ladder. He saved her life. A few days later, the woman went to the firehouse to thank the fireman. She was so grateful for his actions. In time, they fell in love and got married.

Similarly, when we are in need, we cry out for God to save us. It's a legitimate prayer of need. We call upon Him when we are in trouble, and He saves us. Then, we thank Him. This gratitude is true worship. Worship is the adoring, contemplation of God revealed in the Lord Jesus Christ. Worship is all that we are, responding to all that God is. All that we are—body, soul, spirit, mind, will, and emotions—thanking God for all that He is. It is everything in us responding to all that God is.

Our English word worship comes from the word, "worth-ship." We place worth on what we worship. Indeed, we worship what we feel is valuable, meaningful, and amazing. Revelation 5:12 speaks of those around the throne saying with a loud voice, "Worthy is the Lamb that was slain, to receive power and riches and wisdom, and strength and honor and glory and blessing!"

Would you like to take a barometer of your worship? It's a simple test. How much do you love God? How much does He mean to you? Just look at your worship. The way you worship God will tell others what you think of the Lord Jesus Christ. How much does He matter to you? Whatever Jesus is worth to you will show up in your worship.

APPLICATION

What did you think of the fire rescue story? Have you ever had to be rescued from a fire, car wreck, flood, or some other disaster?

_____

_____

_____

_____

_____

How much is Jesus worth to you? How much does He matter to you right now?

_____

_____

_____

_____

_____

Take a few moments to pray and thank God for all He has done for you. Make a list of five ways you want to worship Him today.

_____

_____

_____

_____

_____

_____

_____

Lord, teach me what it is to worship in spirit and in truth.

> Jesus said to her, "Woman, believe Me, the hour is coming
> when you will neither on this mountain, nor in Jerusalem,
> worship the Father. You worship what you do not know;
> we know what we worship, for salvation is of the Jews."
>
> **JOHN 4:21-22**

In the story today, a woman is participating in a theological argument because Jesus is getting very close to her deepest need. Like many people, she is good at changing the subject. Rather than admit the emptiness of her life, she chooses to argue religion with the Son of God. She wants to get an argument going rather than face her pain. In today's society, we do the same thing.

Do you know what the Samaritans did? They rejected all of the Bible, except the first five books of the Bible. The only books they accepted were Genesis, Exodus, Leviticus, Numbers, and Deuteronomy. Then, they rejected all the rest of it. Because of this, the Samaritans were limited in their knowledge. There were many facets of the Bible that they didn't know or understand. One of these facets was worship.

In Samaritan worship, everything was primarily emotional. They worked themselves up into a frenzy when they worshiped. The Jews were led primarily by the Pharisees, and they had all of the Bible, they had all of the prophets, and they had the truth. But, they didn't have the Spirit. The Samaritans' worship was enthusiastic, that is spirited worship. Yet, they didn't have the truth.

Things today are not much different. It seems many churches today have dry, liturgical worship that conveys no emotion, joy, or passion. On the other side, some churches worship with great abandon and energy but have no depth or truth in their services. Some are frozen in formalism; others are frenzied in fanaticism. However, the Bible teaches that there is to be a balance of the two: we are to worship in joyful spirit and rock-ribbed truth. John 4:24 tells us, "God is Spirit, and those who worship Him must worship in spirit and truth."

APPLICATION

Have you ever found yourself changing the subject in a conversation (as the Samaritan woman did) to avoid something personal or unpleasant?

....

....

....

....

Looking at the types of worshipers, which better describes you: frozen in formalism, frenzied in fanaticism, or a balance of the two?

....

....

....

....

Ask God to make you a person who worships in both spirit and in truth. You might write out your prayer.

....

....

....

....

....

....

As I study, teach me more about what it is to be filled with the Spirit.

35

> And do not be drunk with wine, in which is dissipation;
> but be filled with the Spirit, speaking to one another
> in psalms and hymns and spiritual songs, singing
> and making melody in your heart to the Lord.
>
> **EPHESIANS 5:18-19**

How can we begin to be people who truly worship?

To truly worship, we must be born again, regenerated by God the Father. Additionally, we must be activated by the Spirit. You are born from above, and then you worship from within. The Holy Spirit of God comes into you. Jesus teaches that true worship is Spirit-filled worship. In Ephesians 5:18-19 we read, "And do not be drunk with wine, in which is dissipation; but be filled with the Spirit, speaking to one another in psalms and hymns and spiritual songs, singing and making melody in your heart to the Lord."

You cannot worship God apart from being filled with the Holy Spirit. If you're not saved, you cannot worship. If you're not Spirit filled, you will not worship. If you have trouble with worship, if you have no desire to worship, if worship to you is boring and tedious, do you know what that says about you? You're either not saved or not Spirit filled.

So, how does a person become Spirit filled? It's not complicated. To be filled with God's Spirit is to agree with the Spirit as to the desire and purpose of the Spirit. What are the desire and the purpose of the Holy Spirit? To glorify the Lord Jesus Christ.

When your one goal and aim is to glorify Jesus above everything else, when He's more precious to you than silver, more costly than gold, when you want to adore Him, the Holy Spirit of God that is in you will join you and praise will come up out of you. When you get Spirit filled, you'll have to backslide to keep from worshiping. You cannot help but worship. I know when I am Spirit filled, I can't help but love God more. When I'm studying I want to tell God how great He is. And out of my innermost being is flowing a river of living water, of incredible joy.

APPLICATION

Have you been born again, regenerated by the Father? Write out your salvation experience.

....

....

....

....

....

Have you given much thought to being filled by the Spirit? What did you glean from today's devotional?

....

....

....

....

Pray and invite God to fill you up to overflowing with His Spirit. You may want to write out your prayer.

....

....

....

....

....

....

Father, I ask You to teach me to be balanced in my worship.

36

The LORD is near to all who call upon Him,
to all who call upon Him in truth.
PSALM 145:18

Did you ever play on a seesaw as a child? For best results, one child should be on each end of the board. However, when too many children are on one end or one child hops off of the seesaw, the board falls heavily to one side, losing all balance. The ride is most enjoyable when weight is balanced across the board.

Likewise, in the Christian life, we also need balance in our worship. That's where the Bible comes into play. To truly worship in a biblical, healthy way, our worship is to be regulated by the Word of God.

There are churches in which the balance can get off. In some churches, the people want all praise, worship, singing, testifying, and celebration. They avoid Bible teaching at all costs, not wanting to study at all. That's the reason why all true worship is linked with the study of the Word of God. That's why there are pastors and teachers. We need the truth of God's Word to balance all of the emotions in our churches.

Today's verse in Psalm 145:18 reminds us, "The LORD is near to all who call upon Him, to all who call upon Him in truth." In truth. You don't just conjure up a god of your own imagination and then worship him. That's idolatry. Psalm 47:7 says, "For God is the King of all the earth; sing praises with understanding."

If you worship God in spirit without truth, that will make you a fanatic. If you worship God in truth without the Spirit, that will make you a Pharisee. But if you worship God in spirit and in truth, you will have one of the grandest experiences possible. God is Spirit and they that worship Him must worship Him in spirit and in truth.

APPLICATION

Did you ever play on a seesaw as a child? What was your experience like? Ever have someone jump off and leave you hanging (or falling)?

Why do we need the balance of spirit and truth? What does this look like in your church?

As you close your time today, ask God to give you a wonderful balance of spirit and truth in your worship.

Lord, bless these brief moments I'm about to spend in Your Word.

37

> But the hour is coming, and now is, when the true
> worshipers will worship the Father in spirit and truth;
> for the Father is seeking such to worship Him.
>
> **JOHN 4:23**

What makes you want to go to church or Bible study? What draws you there? Is it the fellowship? Or the people? The teaching? The music? Or something else? What do you seek when you attend worship?

Have you ever thought about the idea that God seeks something from our churches and Bible studies? God seeks after true worshipers. Did you come seeking to worship? You don't come to church primarily for what you can get, you come for what you can give. You don't come to church to worship, you bring your worship to church. You've been worshiping all through the week and then we gather corporately to worship together. God is so pleased when we worship Him corporately in spirit and in truth.

Do you know what's wrong with many churches? They think that worship is some sort of spectator sport. They come to be led in worship by a great band or choir, to be taught and inspired by an amazing preacher, and to be encouraged by the worship experience. It's as if the church has become a performance and they are there to be entertained. That is not the way it's supposed to be. The church is not a theatre and we are not the patrons.

Instead, God designed it differently. The people are the involved participants, the preacher is the prompter facilitating and helping them. And Almighty God is the audience. We are the ones who come together gloriously to praise the Lord Jesus Christ. Our job is to give Him honor, glory, and worship.

As today's verse reminds us, "But the hour is coming, and now is, when the true worshipers will worship the Father in spirit and truth; for the Father is seeking such to worship Him" (John 4:23).

APPLICATION

What makes you want to attend church or Bible study? What is typically the draw for you?

....

....

....

....

....

Why do you think so many churches have turned worship into a performance?

....

....

....

....

....

Ask God to make you a person who worships Him no matter where you are. Take a few moments and pray about your involvement in worship.

....

....

....

....

....

....

....

Lord, as I study, reveal where I've allowed distractions into my life to keep me from You.

> "But the hour is coming, and now is, when the true worshipers
> will worship the Father in spirit and truth; for the Father
> is seeking such to worship Him. God is Spirit, and those
> who worship Him must worship in spirit and truth."
>
> **JOHN 4:23-24**

Some very wealthy people were having a christening party for a new baby. And so all of the people came and they were rejoicing in this baby. As they were eating and drinking and laughing, one of the guests asked where the baby was.

The mother's heart just jumped. She thought about the baby. But she'd not heard the baby, not even a whimper, for a while. As she went to the big master bedroom where she had left the baby, she became concerned. Although she had left the little baby on the center of the bed, her guests had tossed their coats across the bed, not noticing the child. In that darkened room, beneath a pile of coats, was the smothered, dead form of a little baby.

Although the people had come to celebrate the christening of the baby, while they were talking, eating, and drinking, the precious child had been smothered beneath their coats. I can't think of anything much more tragic in the natural world than that. Similarly, I can't think of anything much more tragic than for church people to come to attend worship, drink coffee, talk to their friends, sing, and fail to remember Jesus.

How often we fail to give Him glory and just let Him be smothered under all of our activities! God's great heart desires worship. Is God some sort of an egotist that we have to praise Him? That's not it at all. When we worship and enjoy God, He enjoys our worship. Our praise glorifies God.

When you join in with a community of believers, it's your chance to place importance on your relationship with God. Additionally, gathering in worship allows us to show our fellow worshipers how much we value them.

APPLICATION

What did you think of the tragic story that was shared today? Do you think we smother Jesus out of our worship as the story suggests?

....

....

....

....

....

Why do you suppose it's so easy to fail to remember Jesus? Why do we get so distracted by other things and people?

....

....

....

....

....

Take a few moments to pray today. Invite God to show you any ways that you are not remembering and focusing on Jesus in your worship.

....

....

....

....

....

....

Open my heart to understand more of what it means to be born again.

> Therefore, if anyone is in Christ, he is a new creation; old things have passed away; behold, all things have become new.
>
> **2 CORINTHIANS 5:17**

Have you ever wondered why Jesus said in John 3:7, "You must be born again," rather than you must be educated again, or you must be married again, or you must something else again? Why did Jesus choose the one experience of birth to illustrate what happens when a person becomes a Christian? Because your nature is established by your birth.

My physical nature was established by my physical birth. I was born with brown eyes and dark hair and certain physical traits through the genes and the chromosomes that I received through the very nature of my father and my mother. These things were put into me by God. And when I became a new creature, I received the nature of God. When I was born again, I became a new creature. I was made a partaker of the divine nature.

Because of this, I'm now a man in whom Jesus Christ lives. Anything good that you see about me is not of me; that is, not of my old nature. Anything good you see about me is Jesus Christ who now lives in me. I have received, bless God, a new nature. That's one reason I'm not afraid of losing my salvation. I could no more cease to be a child of God than I could cease to be a son of my earthly father. I couldn't be unborn.

Physical birth is a once-in-a-lifetime experience. Spiritual birth is a once-in-a-lifetime experience as well. Truly, I have become a partaker of the divine nature. Some believe this gives us license to sin. That's not true. When you get saved, you become a partaker of the divine nature. And the old nature is indeed still in you. That which is born of the flesh is flesh.

There will be times when I slip, sin, and fail. However, I am a new creation in Christ Jesus. I'm a partaker in a new nature. You are as well if you have been born again.

APPLICATION

What are four or five traits that make you uniquely you? Hair color? Eye color? Personality? Sense of humor?

....

....

....

....

....

Have you ever thought about being born again? What does this mean in spiritual terms?

....

....

....

....

....

If you have not already, take a moment today and invite God to give you a new nature—to make you a new creation. If you know Jesus, take this time to thank Him for the gift of salvation.

....

....

....

....

....

....

....

Open my heart to better understand the battle taking place for my mind.

But I fear, lest somehow, as the serpent deceived
Eve by his craftiness, so your minds may be
corrupted from the simplicity that is in Christ.
2 CORINTHIANS 11:3

Your mind is an amazing thing. The human mind defies description, and there are possibilities and potentialities in your mind that perhaps you're not aware of. I read somewhere that even in a genius like Einstein, a person uses less than one tenth of one percent of the capacity of the human brain. It's like a great, huge computer. But, if a computer were built big enough and well enough to do even some of the things that your mind can do, the Empire State Building would not be big enough to contain it, and it would take the waters of Niagara to cool it.

Neuroscientists have studied the way in which our brains process information and found that what we think about affects us not only emotionally but also physically. Changes in thinking actually change the brain and can promote behavioral change. In other words, we continually rewire our brains with our thinking. Scripture puts it this way in Proverbs 23:7a, "For as he thinks in his heart, so is he."

Is it any wonder the enemy of our souls wants us to think about unwholesome things? If Satan can plant an evil thought and encourage us to go on a negative tangent, our amazing brains will take us progressively into darker and darker places. The opposite is true as well. As we focus our thoughts on Jesus Christ, the neurotransmitters in our brains send signals that impact us at the cellular level—propelling us, body and soul, in a positive direction.

Your mind is the valued prize in a battle—an out-and-out war—that is being waged at this very moment. There are cosmic forces fighting for control of your mind! That's why today's verse teaches us to beware because "your minds may be corrupted from the simplicity that is in Christ."

APPLICATION

Have you ever studied or thought about the power of the human mind? What amazes you about our minds?

....

....

....

....

....

Did you know that there is a battle for your mind? When have you sensed this?

....

....

....

....

....

Why not pray and ask God to give you the strength to focus your mind on what is best? Ask Him to protect your mind.

....

....

....

....

....

....

Father, as I read, show me any ways that I have lost my joy and my zeal for You.

41

When I remember these things, I pour out my soul within me. For I used to go with the multitude; I went with them to the house of God, with the voice of joy and praise, with a multitude that kept a pilgrim feast. Why are you cast down, O my soul? And why are you disquieted within me? Hope in God, for I shall yet praise Him for the help of His countenance.

PSALM 42:4-5

The Christian life is to be a life of joy unspeakable and full of glory. Jesus told us in John 15:11, "These things I have spoken to you, that My joy may remain in you, and that your joy may be full." Yet, I believe that there is one thing wrong with many churches today and it is this: that they have a saddening lack of old-fashioned, simply-hearted, New-Testament joy. People come to church like they have come to mourn a corpse rather than to hail a conqueror.

Think about it, people come to church with sad faces and bored spirits. For most, they spent the weekend cheering on their favorite teams, laughing with friends and family, and having fun. Then, they get into a worship service, and they worship without energy, laughter, fun, or passion. When we yell at the games, we are considered fans. But to celebrate in church would be fanatical.

I'm not suggesting that we yell in church. But I do sometimes think that we call ourselves dignified when we are simply lifeless and disinterested. This ought not to be the case. Instead, there ought to be freedom and joy that marks all of our worship times. People should attend services and sense the hope that we have. Those who live and work around us should also notice that there is something different and something positive about our lives.

Perhaps that's why so many unbelievers have no interest in our church or our Savior. When they observe our lives and watch how we live, they sense nothing different or victorious about us at all. Why would they want our Jesus if He hasn't changed our lives or made us better?

APPLICATION

Why do you suppose so many people attend church with somber attitudes?

....

....

....

....

When your friends, neighbors, family members, and co-workers observe the way you live, do you attract them to the Lord Jesus? Why or why not?

....

....

....

....

....

Take a few moments and pray about what you have read today. You might want to write out your prayer.

....

....

....

....

....

....

Lord, teach me more about what it means to be desperate for You.

> In the first year of Darius the son of Ahasuerus, of the lineage
> of the Medes, who was made king over the realm of the
> Chaldeans—in the first year of his reign I, Daniel, understood
> by the books the number of the years specified by the word
> of the LORD through Jeremiah the prophet, that He would
> accomplish seventy years in the desolations of Jerusalem.
> Then I set my face toward the Lord God to make request by
> prayer and supplications, with fasting, sackcloth, and ashes.
>
> **DANIEL 9:1-3**

Prayer is our greatest resource. God is our sure defense and our hope. And the passage today is a guide for us. Daniel prayed in a time of national calamity, and God heard his prayer. We can learn from Daniel's example as we pray for our nation, city, community, and home.

Truly, the hour is desperate. It is time that the saints of our Lord and Savior Jesus Christ wake up and be called to serious prayer. Only believing, repenting prayer can hold back the floodtides of judgment and sin and release the cleansing power of the Lord Jesus Christ upon our personal lives and on our nation.

Additionally, prayer is a form of worship. To turn to God in desperate prayer is to invite God into the challenges, dangers, and issues that we face. Desperate prayer is not ordinary prayer. It is extraordinary prayer. In Daniel's case, we read of the stance that he took to begin his prayer in Daniel 9:3, "Then I set my face toward the Lord God to make request by prayer and supplications, with fasting, sackcloth, and ashes."

To look to Heaven with great passion, great resolve, and sincere hearts is to begin to touch on the power of God. When we get serious, God hears and answers our prayers. As we pour out our hearts to God in desperation, God bends down close to listen. Psalm 34:18 tells us, "The LORD is near to those who have a broken heart, and saves such as have a contrite spirit."

APPLICATION

How have you found prayer to be a great resource for your life? How has God answered your prayers?

....

....

....

....

Have you ever been desperate when you prayed? What caused your desperation? How did you see God work?

....

....

....

....

Take a few moments today and thank God for the way that He bends down to listen when we pray. Thank Him for drawing in close when our hearts are broken.

....

....

....

....

....

....

Lord, reveal to me what it means to pray with passion and fervor.

> In the first year of Darius the son of Ahasuerus, of the lineage of the Medes, who was made king over the realm of the Chaldeans—in the first year of his reign I, Daniel, understood by the books the number of the years specified by the word of the LORD through Jeremiah the prophet, that He would accomplish seventy years in the desolations of Jerusalem. Then I set my face toward the Lord God to make request by prayer and supplications, with fasting, sackcloth, and ashes.
>
> **DANIEL 9:1-3**

How do we pray with more power? One way to take our prayer lives to the next level is to pray with serious concentration. If you re-read verse 3 in the passage above, you read these words from Daniel: "I set my face toward the Lord God to make request by prayer and supplications, with fasting, sackcloth, and ashes."

Have you ever set your face in prayer? Have you ever desperately sought the Lord? Many of us could not even remember what we prayed for this morning or last night. We rattle off our little prayers. But have you set your face to prayer? Have I?

With prayer, it's not the arithmetic of your prayers; how many prayers you pray. It's not the rhetoric of your prayer; how eloquent or beautiful your prayers may be. It's not the geometry of your prayer; how long your prayer may be. It is not the emotion of your prayer; how sweet and juicy your prayer is. It's not the logic of your prayer; how argumentative your prayer. Rather, it is the faith and fervency of your prayer—prayer that gets to God.

If we aren't careful, we will play at the things of God without really being focused. We pray without passion and without a plan. Carelessly, we read the Bible quickly before bed. Fasting is nonexistent, witnessing is not happening, and Bible study is seldom in our lives. We are playing at church. Is it any wonder that we have so little power in our lives? To tap into Heaven, we must set our faces in prayer and desperately seek the Lord.

APPLICATION

Why do you think it's so easy to pray without passion?

....

....

....

....

If you were to be honest with a close friend, how would you rate your walk with the Lord right now? Are you fervent and falling more in love with Jesus? If not, how would you like for things to change?

....

....

....

....

Take a moment and talk to the Father about these things. You may want to write out your thoughts.

....

....

....

....

....

....

Lord, speak to my heart as I read today.

> O Lord, righteousness belongs to You, but to us shame of face, as it is this day—to the men of Judah, to the inhabitants of Jerusalem and all Israel, those near and those far off in all the countries to which You have driven them, because of the unfaithfulness which they have committed against You. O Lord, to us belongs shame of face, to our kings, our princes, and our fathers, because we have sinned against You. To the Lord our God belong mercy and forgiveness, though we have rebelled against Him.
>
> **DANIEL 9:7-9**

Daniel prayed with incredible confidence. He gazed steadfastly at God while glancing at the problems he was facing.

As you listen to the prayer of Daniel the prophet, it is saturated with confidence in Almighty God. Look back to verse 4, "And I prayed to the Lord my God, and made confession, and said, 'O Lord, great and awesome God, who keeps His covenant and mercy with those who love Him, and with those who keep His commandments.'" What a mighty God we serve. Daniel knew this full well, as can we.

Throughout these verses, Daniel mentions the greatness of Almighty God. His prayer is filled with worship and awe of the Lord. Daniel mentions qualities like God's greatness, God's awe, God's power, God's righteousness, and God's mercy. It is impossible to see Who our great God is and not want to pray. Aren't you glad that we have a God to whom we can pray?

So, how can we pray with more of a sense of confidence? We can begin our prayer times with praise. As we approach each day and the many challenges that we face, we can pause, look to Heaven, and thank God for His greatness, awe, power, righteousness, and mercy. Further, we can tell Him how thankful we are for all of the sweet blessings He sends to us. For just a moment each morning, we take our gaze and fix it upon Jesus. This will transform us and our days!

APPLICATION

Would you say that you are a person who prays with great confidence? Why or why not?

....

....

....

....

In the space below, write down ten ways you see the greatness of God in your life. What has He done in your life, through your life, and with your life?

....

....

....

....

....

....

....

Now, go back over the list you just made above, and praise God for every single one of these things.

....

....

....

Open my heart to understand the pure satisfaction that You offer.

> Jesus answered and said to her, "Whoever drinks of this water will thirst again, but whoever drinks of the water that I shall give him will never thirst. But the water that I shall give him will become in him a fountain of water springing up into everlasting life." The woman said to Him, "Sir, give me this water, that I may not thirst, nor come here to draw."
>
> **JOHN 4:13-15**

Have you ever been outside, perhaps working in the garden or bicycling or playing touch football or cutting the grass or something else, and become very thirsty?

What do you want to drink to quench that thirst? Possibly you think a soda will help to quench your thirst. So you drink the soda and go back out to work or play again. But, after a while, you are thirsty again. What do you want to drink now? Perhaps a glass of water? Isn't it amazing how satisfied you feel after you drink the water? It just hits the spot and satisfies your thirst.

Why is this? Typically, the soda is filled with artificial colors and artificial flavors and lots of sugar. It just doesn't have that touch of authenticity and reality. But the water is different. To drink fresh, cool water is to be deeply satisfied.

In like manner, we do the same thing in our spiritual lives. We try to satisfy our thirst with things that are artificially colored and artificially sweetened. What we need is the water of life; we need to learn how to worship God in spirit and in truth. Today's passage reminds us of this very truth. Jesus was talking to a woman who had found her life to be unsatisfying.

As she talks to Jesus about water, He shares this truth with her in John 4:13-14, "Whoever drinks of this water will thirst again, but whoever drinks of the water that I shall give him will never thirst. But the water that I shall give him will become in him a fountain of water springing up into everlasting life." True satisfaction for our souls is only found in one place: in a personal relationship with Jesus Christ. Everything else is just artificial and unsatisfying.

APPLICATION

When you get really hot and thirsty, what is your favorite thing to drink? Why?

....

....

....

....

....

How is Jesus like fresh water that satisfies? How has the Lord Jesus brought satisfaction into your life?

....

....

....

....

....

Take a few moments and thank the Lord for the true satisfaction He brings.

....

....

....

....

....

....

....

As I study today, I ask You to strengthen and grow my love for You.

> "And you shall love the LORD your God with all your heart, with all your soul, with all your mind, and with all your strength. This is the first commandment."
>
> **MARK 12:30**

Do you know what the first commandment is? The first commandment is not the great commission, the first commandment is this, "you shall love the LORD your God with all your heart, with all your soul, with all your mind, and with all your strength." This is the first commandment; there is nothing more important than just loving God. Nothing!

In Proverbs 23:26, we read where the writer of Proverbs encourages his son to give him his heart. He says to his son, "My son, give me your heart, and let your eyes observe my ways." I believe that Solomon wrote this and is speaking to his own son. Also, I believe that it is indicative of what God through Solomon is saying to every one of us. God wants us to give Him our hearts.

There is only one thing that God wants, and that is our hearts. God needs nothing apart from you or nothing from you apart from your love. It is your love that God wants.

You see, if you were to give God your riches, you couldn't make God any richer because He owns it all. If you were to give God your strength you couldn't make God any stronger because He is omnipotent. If you were to give God your wisdom you couldn't make God any wiser because God is omniscient. If you were to give God your glory you couldn't make God any more glorious, for God is all glorious. If you were to give God your power, God would be no more powerful because He is already all-powerful.

What I'm saying dear friend, the thing that God wants from you is your love. The Father seeks those who worship Him. Will we give Him our hearts in loving worship? Will we listen to Him, spend time with Him, and develop a deeper and more meaningful relationship with Him?

APPLICATION

Why do you think that the first commandment is for us to love God? Why does this matter?

....

....

....

....

....

How is your love for God right now? Does He have your whole heart? If not, what needs to change? What adjustments need to be made in your life?

....

....

....

....

....

Why not take a few moments to pray today and give God your life afresh and anew?

....

....

....

....

....

....

Lord, help me to grasp the power of praise in my own life.

> "And you shall love the LORD your God with all your heart, with all your soul, with all your mind, and with all your strength. This is the first commandment."
>
> **MARK 12:30**

Years ago, I talked to a man about Jesus. He listened for a bit and then began to argue with me. He puffed out his chest and told me what a great guy he was. Bragging about his goodness, he shared how he didn't lie, cheat, or steal. He provided for his family and was good to his wife. Then he actually told me that he had not sinned; there was nothing that needed saving in his life. My response was simple. I told him that the sin in his life was high treason against the King of kings for refusing to worship God.

Truly, there is no greater sin. The first commandment tells us to love God with all of our heart, soul, mind, and strength. To break this commandment is the greatest sin. It's a greater sin than rape, a greater sin than murder, and a greater sin than perversion to fail to worship God. God desires it, God deserves it, and God demands it.

It's about time that we came back to see how important worship is because God demands it. Even more, God is not going to bless anybody who doesn't worship Him. You've got to learn how to worship if you want power.

Do you remember the story of King Jehosophat in 2 Chronicles 20? When the people started to worship, God started to move. King Jehosophat and the armies of Mohab surrounded the armies of Israel and the people were afraid. Jehosophat prayed and asked God what to do. God's answer was to have the people praise Him. They were instructed to sing and give praise to God. When they followed these instructions, God gave them the victory! When we begin to worship, then God begins to work.

If it seems like when you pray your prayers are dry and powerless, try worship and praise and you'll have an ocean to swim in. Worship the Lord, praise the Lord, and give Him glory.

APPLICATION

Can you relate to the man in the story who felt he was too good to be saved? Maybe you've talked to people like this when you were trying to tell them about Jesus?

....

....

....

....

....

Why do you suppose praise and worship bring about such victory? Why is it so powerful?

....

....

....

....

....

Close your time today in praise. In the space below, write out a prayer of praise to God for who He is and for what He has done.

....

....

....

....

....

....

....

Lord, bless these moments that I spend in Your Word today.

48

> "Our fathers worshiped on this mountain, and you Jews say that in Jerusalem is the place where one ought to worship." Jesus said to her, "Woman, believe Me, the hour is coming when you will neither on this mountain, nor in Jerusalem, worship the Father. You worship what you do not know; we know what we worship, for salvation is of the Jews."
>
> **JOHN 4:20-22**

Does it matter where we worship? In the story above, Jesus is talking to a woman about places of worship. She asked about whether people should worship God on Mt. Gerizim or in Jerusalem. Jesus explained to the woman that real worship is not tied up in a place, it is tied up in a person.

Of course, church attendance is important, but worship is not tied to a church or an assembly of believers. The Bible teaches us in Hebrews 10:25 to gather together by "not forsaking the assembling of ourselves together; as is the manner of some." However, in worship, there is no ground that is not holy ground. There is no time or place that is sacred and no place where God will not meet with men and women. He is with us always and will never leave us or forsake us.

Unfortunately, many people have their worship tied up in places and buildings and shrines. They think that they have to go to that place to worship God. But they are not worshiping God in this way. Instead, they are worshiping a place. Stained glass, beautiful architecture, wooden pews, and candles may be beautiful, but they are not necessary for us to worship.

When you study the Bible, you'll find out that Abraham worshiped God under a tree. Moses worshiped God by a bush in the wilderness. Noah worshiped God in an ark. Adam worshiped God in a garden. Jonah worshiped God in a fish, Paul worshiped God by the roadside, and Jacob worshiped God with his head upon a stone. We can worship God anywhere. Because it's a matter of the heart, you and I can enjoy God's presence no matter where we worship.

APPLICATION

Does it matter to you where you worship? Do you have some favorite places to spend time with God?

....

....

....

....

....

Why do you think it's so easy to get caught up in the where of worship? Why does this matter so much to some people?

....

....

....

....

....

Right where you are, take a few moments to worship God. Take some time to write out your prayer.

....

....

....

....

....

....

Lord, open the eyes of my heart as I study today.

49

Then I looked, and I heard the voice of many angels around the throne, the living creatures, and the elders; and the number of them was ten thousand times ten thousand, and thousands of thousands, saying with a loud voice: "Worthy is the Lamb who was slain to receive power and riches and wisdom, and strength and honor and glory and blessing!"

REVELATION 5:11-12

What happens when you worship God in spirit? When you worship God in spirit there's liberty; not formalism, nor ritualism, but liberty. 2 Corinthians 3:17 tells us, "Now the Lord is the Spirit; and where the Spirit of the Lord is, there is liberty."

What does freedom look like in worship? There are those who tend toward a formal service. They like things to be reverent and quiet. Still others prefer the music ramped up and the congregation standing with arms raised. Some love trumpets and some like violins. In some churches, there is a lot of noise and fervor, in others, it is somber and more dignified.

Would it surprise you to know that there can be freedom in all these types of worship and many more? Where the Spirit of the Lord is, there is freedom and liberty. When we study worship in the Bible, we find that it's marked with a certain brightness, spontaneity, and joy. On numerous occasions in the Scriptures, we read about tremendous praise occurring, often completely unplanned and unorganized.

One interesting moment of worship takes place in today's verses. It's a heavenly worship service. As thousands and thousands of angels and elders gather around God's throne, tremendous praise breaks out. They begin to cry out in joy, "Worthy is the Lamb who was slain to receive power and riches and wisdom, and strength and honor and glory and blessing!" What a beautiful picture of complete and total freedom in worship!

APPLICATION

What does freedom in worship look like? When was the last time you were part of a service where there was great joy and celebration?

....

....

....

....

....

In your own life, have you had any recent moments of great worship? What took place?

....

....

....

....

....

As you pray today, invite God to give you more and more freedom in your worship of Him.

....

....

....

....

....

....

Lord, show me more about the amazing place called Heaven.

> "Let not your heart be troubled; you believe in God, believe also in Me. In My Father's house are many mansions; if it were not so, I would have told you. I go to prepare a place for you. And if I go and prepare a place for you, I will come again and receive you to Myself; that where I am, there you may be also."
>
> **JOHN 14:1-3**

Gallup took a poll about life after death. They discovered that more than 70% of Americans believe there is a Heaven. Only 60% of those surveyed said they believed in a real place called Hell. But only 4% of those surveyed believed they would likely go to Hell. One old Gospel song has a line that says, "Everybody talkin' 'bout Heaven ain't going there."

Years ago, I talked to a very prominent politician. He was a former governor and had served under several presidents. At one time, this man considered making a run for the presidency. He was wealthy, powerful, and brilliant. On one particular occasion, Pastor D. James Kennedy and I got to meet with this man and talk with him about his spiritual life.

When we asked this affluent politician if he thought he would be going to Heaven after he died, he responded with an affirming yes. When we asked him why he thought God would let him into Heaven, he told us that all of his service and hard work would earn him a ticket through the gates of Heaven. He was full of pride and self-assurance, but he didn't understand anything about God's grace.

Many people are like this politician. They believe that their good works, efforts, and generosity will earn them a spot in Heaven. But that's not how we get into Heaven. The only way to Heaven is through the person of Jesus Christ. To enjoy the privilege of going to Heaven, we must be saved. We must experience a personal relationship with God through Jesus. He is the only way to Heaven. It's laid out so clearly in Romans 10:13, "For whoever calls on the name of the LORD shall be saved."

APPLICATION

If a survey were done today of your close friends and family members, what percent would say that they believe in Heaven? Hell? How many would say they believe they are going to Heaven?

....

....

....

....

What about you? Have you come to the place in your life where you know that if you died, you would go to Heaven? Why do you feel God should let you into Heaven?

....

....

....

....

Close your devotional time with prayer. If you know Jesus, thank Him for the gift of grace. If you aren't sure, why not talk this over with God today? Tell Him you're a sinner, you want to be forgiven, and you trust Jesus' finished work on the cross. Ask Him to save you.

....

....

....

....

Lord, speak to my heart
as I read today.

> "Let not your heart be troubled; you believe in God, believe also in Me. In My Father's house are many mansions; if it were not so, I would have told you. I go to prepare a place for you. And if I go and prepare a place for you, I will come again and receive you to Myself; that where I am, there you may be also."
>
> **JOHN 14:1-3**

Heaven is a real place. In the Bible, we talk of Heaven as being up. We point up to the sky as we talk about Heaven.

So, where is Heaven? Is it up there somewhere? There are those naysayers who will remind us that the Earth is round. As Paul was in Palestine when he wrote, up was in one particular direction. But, when someone is in Australia, their upwards direction would be completely different. It seems that we are all pointing in different directions. How can Heaven be up if everyone is pointing in different directions?

In Bible days, the people believed that the Earth was flat. Up to them was just a direction above this supposed flat earth. Paul and all others would have just been pointing heavenward—as they understood directions.

Additionally, let me tell you this truth. There is only one place on the face of the globe that is always up. Do you know what it is? It's north. Why? Because the north is a fixed position. If you were to take a camera, open the camera lens, and put it on the North Star, it would never change. You can leave the lens open and see all of the other stars rotating around that North Star. But that North Star would never move. That is a fixed position. I believe the Bible teaches that Heaven is north.

Consider the words of Isaiah 14:13 that speak of Satan falling from Heaven. "For you have said in your heart: 'I will ascend into heaven, I will exalt my throne above the stars of God; I will also sit on the mount of the congregation on the farthest sides of the north.'"

APPLICATION

Have you ever thought about where Heaven is located? Where do you think it is? Why?

....

....

....

....

What do you think of the idea of Heaven being north? What makes this a compelling argument?

....

....

....

....

Why not take a minute and thank God for His amazing wisdom in His creation of Heaven?

....

....

....

....

....

....

Lord, help me to apply these insights today as I read.

52

> So we are always confident, knowing that while we are at home in the body we are absent from the Lord. For we walk by faith, not by sight. We are confident, yes, well pleased rather to be absent from the body and to be present with the Lord.
>
> **2 CORINTHIANS 5:6-8**

What happens when a believer dies?

The Bible teaches us that the saved person will immediately go to Heaven. The instant you close your eyes in death, you will be with Jesus. Some religions teach that there is a weigh station or a place between our time on Earth and our time in Heaven. But the Bible does not teach this. There is no time delay between life here on this Earth and new life in Glory. The Scriptures today tell us that "to be absent from the body" is "to be present with the Lord."

Not so long ago I was at the deathbed of my darling mother. I wish you could have known my mother. My mother was an incredible individual, as was my dad. She had the greatest sense of humor—full of wit and one-liners. You could never get ahead of her in a conversation. She had a funny comeback for everything.

As she was taking her last breath, I was there with her. Well into her nineties, she had lived a full life. So had my father. In her final moments of consciousness, she opened her eyes and looked straight upward. I can't prove it, but I have the feeling that she was looking into another world.

It seems that as we get older, the draw to Heaven gets stronger and the call of Heaven gets louder. The Apostle Paul felt the tug toward Heaven and had a constant battle to depart. In Philippians 1:21-23, he said, "For to me, to live is Christ, and to die is gain. But if I live on in the flesh, this will mean fruit from my labor; yet what I shall choose I cannot tell. For I am hard-pressed between the two, having a desire to depart and be with Christ, which is far better."

APPLICATION

Have you ever thought about how quickly a believer will go to Heaven when he or she dies? How does this encourage you?

_____

_____

_____

_____

Are you looking forward to Heaven? Why or why not?

_____

_____

_____

_____

Talk about Heaven with the Lord as you pray today.

_____

_____

_____

_____

_____

_____

_____

As I study about Heaven, I ask You to open my heart to learn and understand.

53

> For to me, to live is Christ, and to die is gain. But if I live on in the flesh, this will mean fruit from my labor; yet what I shall choose I cannot tell. For I am hard-pressed between the two, having a desire to depart and be with Christ, which is far better.
>
> **PHILIPPIANS 1:21-23**

Heaven is going to be a place of absolute perfection. Truly, we know more about what we will not be doing in Heaven than we do about what we will be doing. The Bible tells us in Revelation 21:4, "And God will wipe away every tear from their eyes; there shall be no more death, nor sorrow, nor crying. There shall be no more pain, for the former things have passed away." I believe this is why Paul said in Philippians 1:21, "For to me to live is Christ and to die," listen, "is gain." "To die is gain." Then he said, "I have a desire to depart and be with Christ, which is far better" (v. 23). Gain. No more sin, no sorrow, no suffering, no death, no disease, no doubts. What is Heaven? Heaven is the presence of all that is good. Heaven is the absence of all that is bad.

Can you imagine someone who loved you so much He gave His Son to die for you? That's love, isn't it? "In this is love, not that we loved God, but that He loved us and sent His Son..." (1 John 4:10).

Heaven is all that the loving heart of God would desire. Heaven is all that the incredible mind of God can conceive. Heaven is all the almighty hand of God can create. Put it together: God's love, God's mind, and God's power. And friend, that's Heaven.

No wonder Paul said in 1 Corinthians 2:9, "Eye has not seen, nor ear heard, nor have entered into the heart of man the things which God has prepared for those who love Him." In the Greek language, he's adding superlatives upon superlatives when he's talking about going to Heaven. It's going to be amazingly amazing! Wonderfully wonderful. Perfectly perfect. Beautifully beautiful.

APPLICATION

Have you ever taken the time to think about what Heaven will be like? What do you imagine it is like?

....

....

....

....

Consider this statement: Heaven is all that a loving God would desire. How does this encourage you?

....

....

....

....

Take a few moments to thank God for Heaven and how amazing it will be. You may want to write out your prayer.

....

....

....

....

....

Lord, reveal what You want me to see from our time together today.

> "Let not your heart be troubled; you believe in God, believe also in Me. In My Father's house are many mansions; if it were not so, I would have told you. I go to prepare a place for you. And if I go and prepare a place for you, I will come again and receive you to Myself; that where I am, there you may be also."
>
> **JOHN 14:1-3**

The story is told of a little girl who was blind and had never seen. But a surgeon believed that he could give sight to that child. The parents were willing. So, they did the surgery. After the surgery, the little girl's eyes were bandaged. Then came the time when the bandages were to be removed. Would she be able to see?

As they unwrapped the gauze, took those pads from her precious little eyes, and the doctor told her to open her eyes, this little girl opened her eyes and blinked. The first thing she saw was the face of that doctor. Then the face of a nurse, then the face of her mother. She saw a tear for the first time in her mother's eye, and she said, "I can see."

She looked around at the things in the room that you and I take for granted. Then she went to the window and looked outside. She didn't see the grass; she saw the green grass. She didn't see the sky; she saw the blue sky. She didn't see the flowers; she saw the multi-colored flowers. She ran back to her mother, squeezed her mother, and said, "Mama, Mama, it's beautiful. Oh, Mama, it's beautiful. Mama, why didn't you tell me it was so beautiful?" That mother, through tears of joy, said, "Sweetheart, I tried to tell you, but you had to see it for yourself."

That's what Heaven will be like for us when we finally see it. It is the consummate work of God's creative genius. You and I will love Heaven. Why? Because Jesus said, "I go and prepare a place for you." And Heaven is a place of absolute perfection—perfectly prepared for you and me.

APPLICATION

Imagine someone who has been blind seeing for the first time. What must that be like?

....

....

....

....

When you picture Heaven in your mind, what do you think it will look like? How does it encourage you to know that it will be 10 times better than anything you can imagine?

....

....

....

....

Take a few moments to pray and thank God for the amazing ways He is preparing Heaven for you.

....

....

....

....

....

....

Father, I ask You to encourage me as I spend time with You today.

55

> "Father, I desire that they also whom You gave Me may be with Me where I am, that they may behold My glory which You have given Me; for You loved Me before the foundation of the world."
>
> **JOHN 17:24**

What do you think will be the very best part of all about Heaven? Seeing loved ones? No more tears? No more pain or death?

Have you ever thought about this fact: Jesus is the crowning glory of Heaven? Heaven is not primarily a place; Heaven is a person. Jesus said, "I go and prepare a place for you...that where I am, there you may be also" (John 14:3). I'm looking forward to being with Jesus, are you? Honestly, if you're not looking forward to being with Jesus, you may not enjoy Heaven very much. If you're just waiting for an eternal vacation or something like that, you're not going to like Heaven.

When I come home after a trip, I don't burst through the door and run over and hug the lamp or the television or my recliner. Instead, I want to see my wife and throw my arms around her. For home to me is my wife, Joyce. Where she is, is where I want to be. She makes my home, home. Truly, Jesus is what makes Heaven, Heaven. To be with Jesus in Heaven is to be home.

One of the great prayers that Jesus prayed is found in John 17:24. He is praying, "Father, I desire that they also whom You gave Me may be with Me..." When we step over into glory, we will see the face of Jesus and behold His glory. To be face to face with Christ my Savior, it will be worth it all when we see Jesus.

Perhaps you remember the old hymn, "It Will Be Worth It All"? The chorus goes like this: "*It will be worth it all when we see Jesus! Life's trials will seem so small when we see Christ. One glimpse of his dear face, all sorrow will erase. So, bravely run the race till we see Christ*" (song lyrics were written by Esther Kerr Rusthoi).

APPLICATION

Why is Jesus such a big part of Heaven? What do you think it will be like to see Him face to face?

_____

_____

_____

_____

_____

Are you looking forward to Heaven? Are you excited about seeing Jesus? If so, why? If not, why not?

_____

_____

_____

_____

_____

Take a few moments and pray about how you feel about Jesus. Invite God to give you a greater love for Jesus and a desire to know Him better than you do right now.

_____

_____

_____

_____

_____

_____

_____

Open my heart to reveal any truth You want to reveal to me today.

> And I said to him, "Sir, you know." So he said to me, "These are the ones who come out of the great tribulation, and washed their robes and made them white in the blood of the Lamb."
>
> **REVELATION 7:14**

Who is going to Heaven? The Bible gives us a very clear answer to this question: only the redeemed are going to Heaven. To go to Heaven, you must be born again. Born from above. You've had an earthly birth, now you need a heavenly birth. And if you're heavenly born, you'll be heavenly bound. Again, if you are Heaven-born, you'll be Heaven-bound. Those in Heaven are those who have been washed by the blood of the Lamb.

Some people believe that their denomination will get them to Heaven. They take great confidence in church affiliation. No denomination ever got anyone to Heaven. Being a good Baptist, Methodist, Catholic, or Lutheran will not earn Heaven for you.

Some feel like their good works will get them to Heaven. They are kind, good to their families, hard-working, pay their taxes, and obey the law. Surely, they are good enough to get into Heaven. But good works do not earn Heaven. The Bible tells us in Romans 3:10, "There is none righteous, no, not one."

Also, some believe that they will get to Heaven on the coattails of their godly parents or grandparents. Having Christian family members will not ensure Heaven for us. Each individual must come into a personal relationship with Jesus for himself. You will not be invited into Heaven because your mother or grandmother is there.

So, how does a person enter Heaven? You must receive Christ and His atoning blood for your sin. Your name must be written in the Lamb's Book of Life. Indeed, John closes the Book of Revelation talking about Heaven: "But there shall by no means enter it anything that defiles, or causes an abomination or a lie, but only those who are written in the Lamb's Book of Life" (Revelation 21:27).

APPLICATION

Who do you believe will be in Heaven? Who is God going to allow to enter?

....

....

....

....

Are you going to Heaven when you die? Why will God let you enter in?

....

....

....

....

Why not pray and talk these things over with God today? If you know Him, thank Him for your salvation. If you aren't sure, you can be. Tell Him you're a sinner, you want to be forgiven, and you trust Jesus' finished work on the cross. Receive Jesus and invite Him to save you.

....

....

....

....

....

....

Lord, as I read about Jesus,
I ask for new insights today.

> While the Pharisees were gathered together, Jesus asked
> them, saying, "What do you think about the Christ? Whose Son
> is He?" They said to Him, "The Son of David." He said to them,
> "How then does David in the Spirit call Him 'Lord,' saying: 'The
> LORD said to my Lord, "Sit at My right hand, till I make Your
> enemies Your footstool"'? If David then calls Him 'Lord,' how is
> He his Son?" And no one was able to answer Him a word, nor
> from that day on did anyone dare question Him anymore.
>
> **MATTHEW 22:41-46**

Who is Jesus? And, what makes Him so special? Let me start by saying clearly and plainly that Jesus is God. Now, if you don't believe this, you can't be right about anything else. Jesus Christ is God in human flesh. If Jesus Christ is not God, Jesus Christ is a liar and an imposter. Truly, Jesus is God.

If Jesus Christ is a man, and only a man, He's a liar. We ought to say, "If Jesus Christ is a man, and only a man, I say that of all mankind, He is a liar for leading so many astray." But He's not a liar. He is the Son of God, the Savior of the world.

When you come to Jesus Christ, you just can't be careless about Him. You can't just tip your hat to Jesus and go on your way. Instead, you're on the horns of a trilemma. Jesus Christ was one of three things. Either He was a liar, or a lunatic, or the Lord. Either He knew He was not God and pretended to be, or else He was not God but thought He was and was a lunatic, or else He was what He claimed to be. Either He was a deceiver, deceived, or deity. Liar, lunatic, or Lord. He's one of the three. Now, you make up your mind. Mine is already made up.

In the days when Jesus walked on this Earth, He asked His disciples who they thought He was. Often, He posed challenging questions to His followers to see what they believed. Perhaps we should consider His questions as well today. If Jesus were to ask you these questions, how might you answer Him? From Matthew 22:42: "What do you think about the Christ? Whose Son is He?"

APPLICATION

Have you ever thought about the trilemma of Jesus Christ? Is He a liar, a lunatic, or Lord? Why?

....

....

....

....

....

If He were to ask you these questions, how would you answer? What do you think about Christ? Whose Son is He?

....

....

....

....

....

Why not take a few minutes and pray about these matters? Talk over any questions or concerns you may have with the Lord.

....

....

....

....

....

....

Lord, I ask You to give me a healthy reverence for Your name.

58

> The voice of one crying in the wilderness: "Prepare the way of the LORD; make straight in the desert a highway for our God."
>
> **ISAIAH 40:3**

The name *Jehovah* is the name for God that's used in the Bible more than 7,000 times. If you have an American Revised Version, you read the word Jehovah. In the King James' Version in the Old Testament, you read the word, Lord. But both these words are translated from the same Hebrew word, *Jehovah* or *LORD*.

If you have a King James' Version, in the Old Testament every place that you read *LORD*, you can just simply say *Jehovah*. It means the same thing. The Old Testament Jewish leaders never spoke this word in audible tones. When they came to the word Jehovah, they shut their eyes, they bowed their heads, and they worshiped. The congregation did the same thing.

When a scribe was very carefully copying the Bible, writing meticulously, he did an interesting thing. When he would come to this word, *Jehovah*, he would lay down that pen and go and get a brand-new pen just to write the name *Jehovah*. How much reverence they had for this name for God!

Jehovah was the name that was used for God when God was in a relationship with His people, when God was dealing with His people. We could call it the fellowship name for God. This word is used in Isaiah 40:3 when the prophet declares, "Prepare the way of the LORD; make straight in the desert a highway for our God." The word *LORD* is *Jehovah*.

In the New Testament, we read this name of God in Matthew 3:3. In this verse, Matthew writes, "For this is he who was spoken of by the prophet Isaiah, saying: The voice of one crying in the wilderness: 'Prepare the way of the LORD; Make His paths straight.'" John the Baptist prepared the way for Jehovah—for the coming of the Lord Jesus Christ.

APPLICATION

Have you ever heard the word *Jehovah* used? What did you know about this word before you read today's devotional?

....

....

....

....

Would you say that you have a healthy reverence for God and His name? Why or why not?

....

....

....

....

Why not pray today and tell God how much you admire and respect Him? You can use the space below to write out a prayer if you'd like.

....

....

....

....

....

....

Open my heart to learn all
You want me to learn today.

59

> And as they went to tell His disciples, behold, Jesus met them, saying, "Rejoice!" So they came and held Him by the feet and worshiped Him. Then Jesus said to them, "Do not be afraid. Go and tell My brethren to go to Galilee, and there they will see Me."
>
> **MATTHEW 28:9-10**

In the Scriptures today, we read the story of the resurrected Jesus seeing His disciples for the first time after His resurrection. When they saw Him, they bowed down, grabbed His feet, and they worshiped Him. Why did they do this? And why did Jesus allow them to do this?

Remember, earlier in Jesus's ministry, when Satan tried to get Jesus to sin. We read in Luke 4:8 where Jesus answered him, "Get behind Me, Satan! For it is written, 'You shall worship the LORD your God, and Him only you shall serve.'" Nobody is to be worshiped but God. He is the only One worthy of worship. If Jesus were not God, do you think He would have allowed His disciples to bow at His feet? Do you think that Jesus would tolerate such idolatry?

On another occasion, Thomas fell at the feet of Jesus and worshiped. We read this account in John 20:27-28, "Then He said to Thomas, 'Reach your finger here, and look at My hands; and reach your hand here, and put it into My side. Do not be unbelieving, but believing.' And Thomas answered and said to Him, 'My Lord and my God!'"

There is only one God whom we worship. But Jesus received adoration that belonged only to God. The ultimate sin is idolatry, and Jesus would never have encouraged it. He must be God if He allowed men and women to bow at His feet and worship Him. This is one of the ways that we know He is God, because He allowed people to adore Him and give Him praise.

The words to a familiar chorus come to mind. Maybe you remember the song "He is Lord" by Rev. Marvin Frey? "*He is Lord. He is Lord! He is risen from the dead and He is Lord! Ev'ry knee shall bow; ev'ry tongue confess that Jesus Christ is Lord.*"

APPLICATION

Have you ever thought about the idea that Jesus allowed people to worship Him while He was here on Earth? Why is this significant?

....

....

....

....

....

What makes you want to worship God? What are you grateful for? What do you appreciate that Jesus has done for you?

....

....

....

....

....

Take a few moments to pause and worship Jesus. Write out your prayer.

....

....

....

....

....

....

....

Lord, speak to my heart
as I read today.

> Now to Him who is able to do exceedingly abundantly
> above all that we ask or think, according to the power
> that works in us, to Him be glory in the church by Christ
> Jesus to all generations, forever and ever. Amen.
>
> **EPHESIANS 3:20-21**

What makes Jesus special? Unique? Unlike any other? What is Jesus able to do that no one else can do? In the first place, Jesus is able to save because He is God. In Hebrews 7:25, the Bible teaches us, "He is also able to save to the uttermost those who come to God through Him, since He always lives to make intercession for them."

No matter what you are dealing with, Jesus can save you. No matter how deep or great your sin, Jesus can save you. No matter how heavy a burden you carry, Jesus can save you. No matter how strong your temptations, Jesus can save you. You can't go too high or too low for Him to reach you. You can't go too far away for Him to reach you. There is nothing that can keep Jesus from saving you. He's able to save you and save you to the uttermost.

Not only is Jesus special because He can save, but also because He can subdue. In Philippians 3:21, we read about Jesus, "Who will transform our lowly body that it may be conformed to His glorious body, according to the working by which He is able even to subdue all things to Himself." There's no problem you have that He's not the Master over. He is Lord and capable of doing all things for you, in you, and with you. In Jeremiah 32:27, the Lord asks, "Behold, I am the LORD, the God of all flesh: is there any thing too hard for me?"

Another attribute of Jesus that stands out is His ability to satisfy our souls. In Ephesians 3:20, we read, "Now to Him who is able to do exceedingly abundantly above all that we ask or think, according to the power that works in us." Whatever your need, He can meet it; I don't care what it is. He's able to do exceedingly abundantly more. Jesus, our Savior, is able to save, able to subdue all things, and able to satisfy.

APPLICATION

When you think about Jesus, what makes Him unique and special? What do you most appreciate about Him?

....

....

....

....

....

How do you need Him to work in your life today? How do you need Him to come through for you?

....

....

....

....

....

Why not pray and invite Jesus to act on your behalf today? Tell Him where you are struggling and how you need His help right now.

....

....

....

....

....

....

....

Lord, increase my appreciation for Jesus as I study today.

61

Let this mind be in you which was also in Christ Jesus, who, being in the form of God, did not consider it robbery to be equal with God, but made Himself of no reputation, taking the form of a bondservant, and coming in the likeness of men. And being found in appearance as a man, He humbled Himself and became obedient to the point of death, even the death of the cross. Therefore God also has highly exalted Him and given Him the name which is above every name, that at the name of Jesus every knee should bow, of those in heaven, and of those on earth, and of those under the earth, and that every tongue should confess that Jesus Christ is Lord, to the glory of God the Father.

PHILIPPIANS 2:5-11

Who is Jesus? Let me describe Him to you using a poem from "The Unique Galilean," edited by Russell V. DeLong, Ph.D.

"To the artist, He's altogether lovely. To the architect, He's the chief cornerstone. To the baker, He's the living bread. To the banker, He's the hidden treasure. To the biologist, Jesus is the life. To the builder, Jesus is the sure foundation. To the doctor, Jesus is the great physician. To the educator, Jesus is the great teacher. To the farmer, He's the Lord of the harvest. To the florist, He's the rose of Sharon. To the geologist, Jesus is the rock of ages. To the jurist, He's the righteous judge. To the jeweler, Jesus is the pearl of great price. To the lawyer, He's my advocate. To the publisher, He's good tidings of great joy. To the philosopher, He is the wisdom of God. To the preacher, He's the Word of God. To the sculptor, He's the living stone. To the statesman, He is the desire of all nations. To the theologian, He is the author and the finisher of our faith. To the traveler, He is the new and the living way. To the sinner, He's the Lamb of God that taketh away the sin of the world. To the Christian, He's the Son of the living God, our Redeemer, and our Lord. And I say hallelujah, what a Savior! Jesus is, indeed, magnificent."

APPLICATION

To which of these descriptions of Jesus can you best relate? Why?

....

....

....

....

....

What three things do you most appreciate about Jesus right now? Write them down.

....

....

....

....

Now, go back and thank Him for these things that you appreciate about Him. If you'd like, write out your appreciation.

....

....

....

....

....

....

....

Open my heart to understand more about how amazing Heaven will be.

And I heard, as it were, the voice of a great multitude, as the sound of many waters and as the sound of mighty thunderings, saying, "Alleluia! For the Lord God Omnipotent reigns! Let us be glad and rejoice and give Him glory, for the marriage of the Lamb has come, and His wife has made herself ready." And to her it was granted to be arrayed in fine linen, clean and bright, for the fine linen is the righteous acts of the saints.

REVELATION 19:6-8

Have you ever been to Niagara Falls or maybe watched the falls online? As you stand and listen to those waters, they just keep coming. Wave after wave of water pours over the top. I wonder if they turn off the fall at night or just allow the water to keep crashing over the rocks. At the falls, there is a crescendo of noise as the water crashes down below. It's a tumultuous sound of this great rushing water.

When is the last time you experienced a thunderstorm? As the storm clouds roll over and the rain pours, lightning begins to flash down from the heavens. Then, you hear great clashes of thunder. Often, it sounds like the angels are bowling up above.

What will our praise be like in Heaven? Imagine putting together the noise, sounds, energy, and excitement of Niagara Falls, a massive thunderstorm, and a loud football stadium. That's what it's going to sound like. Friend, that's going to be some kind of sound. What will our praise be like in Heaven?

Why will this be the case? Because Jesus is reigning. Read Revelation 19:6 again: "And I heard, as it were, the voice of a great multitude, as the sound of many waters and as the sound of mighty thunderings, saying, 'Alleluia! For the Lord God Omnipotent reigns!'" Jesus, who was despised and rejected, looked down upon, and spit upon, is the King of kings and Lord of lords. And every knee shall bow before Him. Then, the shouts of His praise are going to be heard through all of Heaven. It's going to be wonderful.

APPLICATION

Have you ever been to Niagara Falls or a loud waterfall? What was it like? What was the sound like?

Can you imagine our loud and thunderous praise in Heaven? What do you think it will be like?

Why not get a little warm-up on your worship now? Turn on your favorite worship song and sing along at the top of your lungs. (You may want to close the door or sing when you are in your car alone!)

Teach me more today about how to experience more of Jesus.

Behold, He is coming with clouds, and every eye will see Him,
even they who pierced Him. And all the tribes of the earth
will mourn because of Him. Even so, Amen. "I am the Alpha
and the Omega, the Beginning and the End," says the Lord,
"who is and who was and who is to come, the Almighty."

REVELATION 1:7-8

Why does the Bible describe Jesus as the Alpha and Omega? In the Greek alphabet, Alpha is the first letter and Omega is the last. If John were writing the book of Revelation today, he would say that Jesus is God's complete alphabet; He is A to Z. This means that He is the beginning and the end. He's the first, the last, and all the letters in between.

The other day, I counted the books in my library. Literally, I have thousands of books. And all of those books are put together with just 26 letters. They are arranged in different ways. However, all of the wisdom in those books, all of the thoughts in those books, are contained in just 26 letters. Similarly, Jesus is Alpha and Omega.

When you've said Jesus, you've said it all. Jesus is the accumulated wisdom of Almighty God. He is the beginning! He is the end! He is all the letters in between. He is God's first word. He is God's full word. He is God's final word! He is the One who is omniscient. He is Alpha and Omega.

How does this truth impact you personally? You'll never need anything more than Jesus. Don't get the idea that all you need is salvation. There is so much more in Christ. Truly, you'll never need more than Jesus. You'll never go beyond Him. But you can have more of Jesus. You can go deeper into Jesus. You should seek nothing more, and friend, you should settle for nothing less than all of Jesus.

To have more of Jesus, spend time daily with Him. Pray and talk to Him. Read and study the Bible. Get plugged into a great church. Spend time with others who know Him and love Him. You can also learn more about Jesus through podcasts, inspirational books, and godly mentors.

APPLICATION

Have you ever thought about the truth that Jesus is the Alpha and Omega? What does this mean for you?

....

....

....

....

....

Do you have as much of Jesus as you want to have? How might you experience more of Him? What are two or three things you can do to know Him better?

....

....

....

....

Take a few moments and share your heart with the Lord. Talk things over with Him. Use the space below to write out a prayer.

....

....

....

....

....

....

Lord, turn Your searchlight into my life and show me all I need to see today.

"Behold, I send My messenger, and he will prepare the way before Me. And the Lord, whom you seek, will suddenly come to His temple, even the Messenger of the covenant, in whom you delight. Behold, He is coming," says the LORD of hosts. "But who can endure the day of His coming? And who can stand when He appears? For He is like a refiner's fire and like launderers' soap. He will sit as a refiner and a purifier of silver; He will purify the sons of Levi, and purge them as gold and silver, that they may offer to the LORD an offering in righteousness. Then the offering of Judah and Jerusalem will be pleasant to the LORD, as in the days of old, as in former years."

MALACHI 3:1b-4

Malachi preached at the close of the Old Testament, at the close of the dispensation, at the close of an age. At this time, the people had a form of religion, but they denied the power thereof. They were superficial at best, completely unaware of their needs. Often, they asked the most impudent questions, sometimes sarcastic questions, of God.

Their greatest need was to see their need. These people were not truly worshiping God, and God was not accepting their empty worship. They gave gifts, but God didn't receive them. It was all just superficial and playing at religion.

I heard about a woman who was driving her car one day when the engine just shut off. No matter what she did, she couldn't restart the car. And she knew very little about cars. In a few minutes, a tow truck arrived to take her and the broken-down car to a mechanic. After a few minutes spent inspecting the car, the mechanic reported to her that the car was simply out of gas. Rather cluelessly, she asked if she'd be able to drive it home like that.

Similarly, many believers are just as clueless in today's churches. They've run out of gas and wonder why they have no power, no peace, and no joy. Completely empty, they just press on playing church and living their lives. All religion; no reality. No substance. No fullness.

APPLICATION

How are the people of Malachi's day like the people of our day? What comparisons can you make between the two groups?

....

....

....

....

....

In what ways have you allowed religion to substitute for spiritual substance in your life? Is there anything you need to confess and make right with God today?

....

....

....

....

....

Why not take a few moments to pray about this? Invite God to turn His searchlight on in your life and reveal any areas that need to change.

....

....

....

....

....

....

....

Lord, help me to gain insights into what it means to be refined.

65

> "Behold, He is coming," says the LORD of hosts. "But who can
> endure the day of His coming? And who can stand when
> He appears? For He is like a refiner's fire and like launderers'
> soap. He will sit as a refiner and a purifier of silver; He will
> purify the sons of Levi, and purge them as gold and silver,
> that they may offer to the LORD an offering in righteousness.
> Then the offering of Judah and Jerusalem will be pleasant
> to the LORD, as in the days of old, as in former years."
>
> **MALACHI 3:1-4**

Did you know that God has a purpose for your life? God is aiming at something in your life. When you receive His grace, He's not finished with you. In Malachi 3:2, we read, "But who can endure the day of His coming?" When the Lord comes, what's going to happen to that person you used to be? Do you think God's going to let your old nature remain? When Jesus Christ comes to save you, He also comes to purify you.

There are many names for Jesus in the Bible. He's Prophet, Priest, and King. He's the Wonderful Counselor, Mighty God, Prince of Peace, Everlasting Father. In the New Testament, He's the Great Physician. He's the Vine. He's the Good Shepherd. But I'll tell you something else He is. He is the Refiner. He is the one who wants to refine your life; that is, to take your life like you would take gold ore or silver ore and burn out the dross and the impurities. That's His goal.

Do you know what God's goal for you is? To purify you. Do you know what God is interested in? Not primarily in making you happy. God's goal for you is to make you holy, to make you pure, to purge you, and to purify you. That's what God is doing your life if you're saved. The moment you got saved, God began to work in you to purify you and to make you holy. God is not as interested in your next car or your health or your job or your bank account as you are. He cares about your needs, but much of what we obsess over is not so important to God. Instead, His priority is to make you more like Jesus Christ. His passion is to purify your life.

APPLICATION

Have you ever thought about God's purpose for your life? What sorts of things have you felt like God was leading you to do? Calling you to do?

....

....

....

....

....

Do you think that it matters that God purifies you to make you like Jesus? What might this look like in your life?

....

....

....

....

....

As you pray today, ask God to show you if there are any areas He'd like to refine in you right now. Surrender to His work in your life.

....

....

....

....

....

....

Lord, speak to my heart as I read today about spending time with You.

> My voice You shall hear in the morning, O LORD; in the morning I will direct it to You, and I will look up.
>
> **PSALM 5:3**

Would you like to begin to see God do some miracles in your life? Would you like to see Him work, provide, and open doors as you've never seen Him do? If so, one of the best ways to do this is to give God first place in your life.

What might this look like? To begin with, it will mean waking up and giving Jesus Christ the first thoughts of your day. You'll need to begin looking in the face of Jesus before you get on social media, turn on the TV, get on your phone, or talk to your family and friends. We need to look into God's face and to have communion with the Lord before we have communion with anybody else.

Do you know what's wrong with so many people? They wake up in the morning and they say, "Good lord, it's morning." Instead, they ought to say, "Good morning, Lord." To start the day with God is to enjoy the experience of living the rest of the day with the grace of God stored up in our hearts. To avoid the Lord in the morning is to have to fight your battles powerless all day long.

Remember in the Lord's Prayer where we ask God to, "Give us this day our daily bread"? Wouldn't that be a foolish prayer at the end of the day? Instead, as Psalm 5:3 reminds us, "My voice You shall hear in the morning, O Lord; in the morning I will direct it to You, and I will look up."

The reason that so many of us spin out, sputter out, and give out before the end of the day is that we neglected to spend time with Jesus. When we don't fill up with Him early in the day, we run out of power long before the finish of the day. Truly, we need a quiet time with the Lord every morning. Lamentations 3:22-23 promises us, "The LORD's mercies...are new every morning."

APPLICATION

Why does it make a difference that we spend time with the Lord every morning?

....

....

....

....

....

Do you have time each morning alone with God? How do you spend this time? If not, how might a devotional time with God bring about more power and more miracles in your life?

....

....

....

....

....

Spend a few moments in prayer as you close today. Ask God to give you a greater desire for time alone with Him.

....

....

....

....

....

....

....

Father, I ask You to open my heart to learn more about Your miracles.

> And Elijah said to her, "Do not fear; go and do as you have said, but make me a small cake from it first, and bring it to me; and afterward make some for yourself and your son. For thus says the LORD God of Israel: 'The bin of flour shall not be used up, nor shall the jar of oil run dry, until the day the LORD sends rain on the earth.'" So she went away and did according to the word of Elijah; and she and her household ate for many days. The bin of flour was not used up, nor did the jar of oil run dry, according to the word of the LORD which He spoke by Elijah.
>
> **1 KINGS 17:13-16**

Is there a recipe for a miracle? Is there a way to experience more of God's goodness and power in your life? A way to see more wonderful things take place in, with, and around your life? I believe there is. And I'll give it to you in a very simple form. There are two ingredients to see more miracles in your life.

First, we must be obedient. In 1 Kings 17:15, we read, "She went and did..." The widow did exactly what Elijah told her to do. The Bible doesn't need to be explained nearly so much as it needs to be believed and obeyed. You don't have to have a PhD to figure that out. I call it the simplicity of obedience. That's the first ingredient to allow miracles to happen.

The second ingredient for miracles in your life is the sufficiency of omnipotence. If you take the simplicity of obedience and the sufficiency of omnipotence and mix them together, you're going to have God's miracle. In essence, you give God all you've got, and then He gives you all He has. It's a great deal, a wonderful trade.

Many of us are not seeing God work in our lives because we have never learned the simple secret of putting God first. Matthew 6:33 reminds us, "But seek first the kingdom of God and His righteousness, and all these things shall be added to you." Just as God performed a miracle in the widow's life, He can do the same in yours. God is able. Are you willing to surrender and be obedient?

APPLICATION

Have you personally experienced any miracles in your own life? Share one of these.

....

....

....

....

What do you think prevents you from enjoying more of God's miracles in your life? What would you like to see change?

....

....

....

....

Take a moment to pause and pray. Invite God to do more miraculous things in your life as you surrender to Him.

....

....

....

....

....

Lord, help me to grasp more about what it looks like to worship You.

> God, who made the world and everything in it, since He is Lord of heaven and earth, does not dwell in temples made with hands. Nor is He worshiped with men's hands, as though He needed anything, since He gives to all life, breath, and all things.
>
> **ACTS 17:24-25**

What makes God so amazing? What are some of the traits we know about God? We read about His character in Acts 17:24-25. To begin with, God is the God of all power. You can't corner Him in your temple and you can't put Him on your shelf. Indeed, He is over and above all creation. And He is worthy of our worship. Yet, many people do not worship Him.

In Paul's day, and our day, people worship all sorts of strange things. They will worship sticks and stones and earth and dirt and fire. But God made all of this! He is above all of this! We have Earth Day. Earth Day! No longer Father God, but now we have Mother Earth. That's where we are. But Paul said, "This God, this God made it all! He is above it all." And with that statement, he banished all of the gods of Greece.

Additionally, our God is the God of infinite love. He made us so that we might know and worship Him. In Acts 17:26-27a, the Bible says, "And He has made from one blood every nation of men to dwell on all the face of the earth, and has determined their preappointed times and the boundaries of their dwellings, so that they should seek the Lord."

Why did God make people? God made us to know Him and love Him and worship Him. According to Acts 17:27-28a, "So that they should seek the Lord, in the hope that they might grope for Him and find Him, though He is not far from each one of us; for in Him we live and move and have our being."

God is not some distant, unmoved, impassive God up in Heaven; He is the great God who made you! He breathed into your nostrils the breath of life! He made you a living soul! And He swung this planet in space so it would be a habitation for all of us.

APPLICATION

Have you ever thought about the amazing traits of God? His love, His power, His strength, His might?

....

....

....

....

....

In the space below, list 8-10 traits of God that you admire and appreciate.

....

....

....

....

....

Now, go back over those traits and thank God for His character. Mention each trait to Him and praise Him for it.

....

....

....

....

....

....

....

Open my eyes, Lord, to any sin that would hinder me from worshiping You today.

> Truly, these times of ignorance God overlooked, but now commands all men everywhere to repent, because He has appointed a day on which He will judge the world in righteousness by the Man whom He has ordained. He has given assurance of this to all by raising Him from the dead.
>
> **ACTS 17:30-31**

When you think about God, what comes to mind? How do you describe Him to your friends and family? What stands out about His nature to you? In the Book of Acts, Paul is sharing some of the wonderful attributes of God with his listeners. In the verses today, Paul mentions the infinite purity and absolute righteousness of God. These traits demand that all people repent.

Repentance. This is not a subject we hear much about. In fact, in our world today, how many preachers call people to repentance in their weekly messages? Do you know the message we need to hear today with all of our idolatry, bigotry, and philosophy? We need to hear the word, "Repent!"

The word "repent" is a change of mind that leads to a change of life. Jesus said, in Luke 13:3b, "Unless you repent you will all likewise perish." Our God is a God of purity and holiness who commands that we repent to have fellowship with Him. Because He cannot fellowship with sin, we must repent.

With this in mind, Paul mentions another character trait of our God. God is the God of eternal salvation who raised Jesus from the dead. Yes. God demands repentance but He also offers salvation. We don't just turn from ourselves and our sin, but we also turn to something else, to Someone else. In repentance, we turn our hearts and lives over to Jesus, who saves us. To repent is to make a complete 180-degree turn and go in a completely new, better, and different direction.

Do you need to repent today? Change directions? Do you need to stop going the way you are going and turn around? If so, God stands ready to forgive.

APPLICATION

What do you think of when you think of repentance? What does it mean to repent?

....

....

....

....

....

Do you need to repent today? Change directions? Turn around? Tell God you're a sinner, you want to be forgiven, and you trust Jesus' finished work on the cross. Receive Jesus and invite Him to turn your life around.

....

....

....

....

....

Is there a particular area of your life that needs repentance? Take a few moments to pray about that issue. God always stands ready to forgive!

....

....

....

....

....

....

....

Father, I ask You to teach me more about what I am doing with Jesus.

70

> Pilate said to them, "What then shall I do with Jesus who is called Christ?" They all said to him, "Let Him be crucified!" Then the governor said, "Why, what evil has He done?" But they cried out all the more, saying, "Let Him be crucified!" When Pilate saw that he could not prevail at all, but rather that a tumult was rising, he took water and washed his hands before the multitude, saying, "I am innocent of the blood of this just Person. You see to it." And all the people answered and said, "His blood be on us and on our children."
>
> **MATTHEW 27:22-25**

What will you do with Jesus? No greater question could be asked of any person. This question was asked in Matthew 27. Jesus stood before Pilate, the Roman governor, to be adjudicated and then to be crucified. But Pilate tried to thrust the matter into the crowd by asking the question, "What then shall I do with Jesus who is called Christ?"

Pilate had to make a decision. This question pressed on his heart, and Pilate called out to the crowds to help make the decision. We too must choose what we will do with Jesus. The fact of Jesus Christ is inevitable and unavoidable. There is no way around answering this question.

What will you do with Jesus? It is a pressing question. You will do something with Him. You may ignore Him, but that's doing something with Him. You may adore Him; that's doing something with Him. You may crown Him, you may crucify Him, you may accept Him, you may reject Him, you may believe Him, you may doubt Him, but you will do something with Jesus, isn't that right? You will do something with Jesus.

A beloved old hymn by Joseph Hart shares the message of choosing Jesus this way: "*Come, ye sinner, poor and needy, weak and wounded, sick and sore. Jesus ready stands to save you, full of pity, love, and pow'r. I will arise and go to Jesus. He will embrace me in His arms. In the arms of my dear Savior, oh, there are ten thousand charms.*"

APPLICATION

What stands out to you about the encounter between Pilate and Jesus?

....

....

....

....

....

What have you personally chosen to do with Jesus? Why? Share a little of your story in the space below.

....

....

....

....

....

Take a few moments to consider Jesus. Tell Him how you feel about Him and how much you appreciate Him.

....

....

....

....

....

....

Show me more today about how much You love me.

71

When He comes, in that Day, to be glorified in His saints
and to be admired among all those who believe, because
our testimony among you was believed. Therefore we
also pray always for you that our God would count you
worthy of this calling, and fulfill all the good pleasure
of His goodness and the work of faith with power.

2 THESSALONIANS 1:10-11

I heard about a little boy who sat up all night wondering where the sun went, and finally, it dawned on him. The coming of Jesus is going to be like that. One day Jesus Christ will pull back the curtains of night and pin them with a star. He'll open the doors of the morning and flood the world with the sunlight of His presence. What a day that will be! The Lord Jesus is coming again.

When we look at 2 Thessalonians 1:10a, we read, "When He comes, in that Day, to be glorified in His saints and to be admired." Focus on the word "admired." The word "admired" means: to be wondered at. It has the idea of awe, wonder. When we see Jesus, we're not going to see Him as a baby with His little dimpled feet there in the straw. He will come to be glorified, and oh, how we will wonder, how we will admire Him.

What will we wonder at when we see Him? One of the traits that will cause us to wonder is His transforming love. In verse 10, we read, "When He comes, in that Day, to be glorified in His saints..." His saints. Who do you think those saints are going to be? They're going to be those who were stubborn, God-hating, unbelieving, wicked, lascivious people who have been transformed. They are those of us who name the name of Christ.

There are going to be those who were once ignorant and blind, who stumbled in the darkness and finally saw the light. These are His saints. They are going to be those who were demonized by sex and drugs and greed. But now they are going to be like Jesus. When we see them with Jesus, there will not be a vestige of sin, not a spot or a wrinkle. That's transforming love. That's the wonder of Jesus and His second coming.

APPLICATION

What do you imagine it will be like when Jesus comes again? What will it look like, sound like, and feel like?

....

....

....

....

....

How has the transforming love of Christ changed you? How are you different since meeting Jesus?

....

....

....

....

As you pray today, thank God for the wonder of His transforming love in your life.

....

....

....

....

....

....

Lord, show me any ways that I have lost my song and my joy.

72

> By the rivers of Babylon, there we sat down, yea,
> we wept when we remembered Zion. We hung our
> harps upon the willows in the midst of it.
>
> **PSALM 137:1-2**

Author Max Lucado tells the story of a parakeet named Chippy. Chippy had something happen to him that completely changed his world. One second he was peacefully perched in his cage; the next he was sucked in, washed up, and blown over. The problems began when Chippy's owner decided to clean Chippy's cage with a vacuum cleaner. She removed the attachment from the end of the hose and stuck it in the cage.

Just as she placed the vacuum hose into Chippy's cage, the phone rang. She turned to pick it up. Before she could even greet the other person on the phone, she heard a loud slurping sound. Chippy got sucked into the vacuum. The bird owner gasped, put down the phone, turned off the vacuum, and opened the bag. There was Chippy still alive but stunned. Since the bird was covered with dust and soot, she grabbed him and raced to the bathroom, turned on the faucet, and held Chippy under the running water. Then realizing that Chippy was soaked and shivering, she did what any compassionate bird owner would do—she reached for the hairdryer and blasted the pet with hot air. Poor Chippy never knew what hit him.

A few days after the trauma, the reporter who had initially written about the event contacted Chippy's owner to see how the bird was recovering. The bird's owner told the reporter that Chippy didn't sing anymore. He would just sit and stare. No wonder! All in one day, he was sucked in, washed over, and blown out with hot air. It seems that he had lost his song.

You know, there are a lot of Christians who have done that. They've lost their songs. Life has sucked them in, washed them over, and blown them out. And they no longer sing. Can you relate? Has the pain and craziness of life stolen your joy, your light, and your spark? If so, you can get it back.

APPLICATION

Have you ever felt like the bird in the story? Chippy? What happened to make you feel this way?

....

....

....

....

Why do you suppose we so quickly allow the storms of life to steal our songs? Are you still singing today or have you lost your song?

....

....

....

....

Pray and invite God to bring back your song, your hope, and your joy again today. Take time to write out your prayer.

....

....

....

....

....

....

Lord, bless these moments
I'm about to spend in
Your Word today.

73

By the rivers of Babylon, there we sat down, yea, we wept
when we remembered Zion. We hung our harps upon the
willows in the midst of it. For there those who carried us away
captive asked of us a song, and those who plundered us
requested mirth, saying, "Sing us one of the songs of Zion!"

PSALM 137:1-3

Do you have, at this moment, joy unspeakable? Is there a song in your heart? Was there a song in your heart and has it gone now? Has your song been stolen? Has something taken your song away from you? That's what happened to the children of Israel. God gave them a land and God gave them a law and God gave them a Lord. But in disobedience they defiled the land, they defied the law, they denied the Lord. And when they did, God raised up the Babylonians to carry them away to Babylon. They lived there in captivity. They lived there in sadness, and their song was gone. Psalm 137:1-3 refers to this season in their lives. Here are people who had lost their song. They had gotten into captivity and the song was gone.

In the Christian life, there are three categories of people. Some still have a song in their lives. They have a melody in their hearts and are singing. These people have peace that passes understanding. They have joy unspeakable and full of glory. Then there are those who once had the song. But they have been taken captive. They may be able to cover up the pain and the sadness so that no one can see the pain. But God sees into the depths of the heart. And you know the truth may be hard to face today. Perhaps you once had the song, but you've lost it. You've been taken captive by the world, the flesh, and the devil.

The third category of people includes those who have never heard the song. You don't even know what I'm talking about because you've never been delivered. You've never been saved. You're drawing your breath, drawing your salary, fighting to live, and living to fight, and on your way to Hell. You've never known the song.

APPLICATION

As you read the story of the children of Israel living in captivity and losing their joy, what do you think this must have been like for them?

....

....

....

....

....

Looking at the three categories of people mentioned today, which are you? Do you have a song? Have you lost your song? Have you ever known the song?

....

....

....

....

....

As you pray today, talk about your song status with God. Ask Him to show you the truth about your current situation.

....

....

....

....

....

....

....

Lord, reveal to me any areas in which I am not following You.

74

> Now great multitudes went with Him. And He turned and
> said to them, "If anyone comes to Me and does not hate his
> father and mother, wife and children, brothers and sisters,
> yes, and his own life also, he cannot be My disciple."
>
> **LUKE 14:25-26**

Would you like to be a disciple of Jesus Christ? The answer is not as easy as you may think. Discipleship costs. Salvation is free, but discipleship costs. Are you willing to pay the price?

If I had a thousand lives, I'd give them all to Jesus. It pays over and over and over and over and over again. I'm always in debt to the Lord Jesus. But may I be honest and tell you something else? It also costs to serve Jesus. It costs every day. It costs every step of the way. And today, we want an air-conditioned, upholstered, streamlined faith. Many of us don't want to pay the price to be a disciple of Christ.

In Luke 14, we read the conditions for becoming a true disciple of Jesus. Luke 14:25-26 says, "Now great multitudes went with Him. And He turned and said to them, 'If anyone comes to Me and does not hate his father and mother, wife and children, brothers and sisters, yes, and his own life also, he cannot be My disciple.'"

Think about this...the crowds were following Jesus. Jesus had great multitudes following after Him. He was at the zenith of His ministry. Enormously popular, people were clamoring after Him.

And what does He do? He throws out a curveball to the crowd. Instead of doing some sensational miracle, He speaks the truth. Instead of watering down His teaching with user-friendly evangelism, He boldly speaks to the people. His words must have seemed shocking to the crowd.

To follow Jesus comes with a great cost.

APPLICATION

When you look around at your friends, co-workers, and family members, do you see many true followers of Christ? Who are they? How are they different?

....

....

....

....

....

What about in your own life? Are you following Jesus no matter the cost? Are you a true disciple of His? If not, what changes might you need to make?

....

....

....

....

....

Why not take a few moments and pray about this? Invite God to show you how you can follow Jesus with more passion and commitment.

....

....

....

....

....

....

....

Lord, teach me as I read today.

75

Now great multitudes went with Him. And He turned and
said to them, "If anyone comes to Me and does not hate his
father and mother, wife and children, brothers and sisters,
yes, and his own life also, he cannot be My disciple."

LUKE 14:25-26

What does a true disciple of Jesus Christ look like? Are there some characteristics that mark the life of a person who wholeheartedly follows Him? Let me share two traits that stand out about a person in love with the Savior.

First, a true disciple wants to worship at any cost. Again, there's no fine print here in the contract. Jesus Christ must come before personal relationships. You're called upon to hate father, mother, wife, children, and brethren. In other words, you must love Jesus more than anyone else. You are called to make Jesus the supreme focus of your life.

Secondly, we must put Jesus before our personal reputations. In Luke 14:26, the Bible says, "And his own life also." You are not even to love yourself more than you love the Lord Jesus Christ. To be a disciple of Jesus Christ, you have to take yourself off the throne and enthrone Jesus Christ.

In many modern churches, the theme is self-fulfillment, self-realization. Our churches have become a sort of a cafeteria line, where we just go by and pick up things that are going to make us feel better about ourselves. Now I hope that you have a good self-image, a healthy self-image, but if it comes between me and Jesus, I must say no to myself and yes to Jesus Christ.

Are you willing to say, "Lord Jesus, I put You first, in spite of my own reputation, my own fulfillment, what people think of me?" To be a true disciple of Jesus Christ, we must be willing to put Him ahead of ourselves, our plans, our dreams, our hopes, our desires, and our wishes. As Jesus taught in Matthew 6:33, in the Sermon on the Mount, "But seek first the kingdom of God and His righteousness, and all these things shall be added to you."

APPLICATION

Would you agree with the two traits that stand out about a person in love with the Savior? Why or why not?

....

....

....

....

....

When you examine your own life, how do you do in the area of discipleship? Do you worship at any cost? Do you put Jesus before your family, friends, and yourself?

....

....

....

....

....

Take a few moments to pray over these things. Allow God to show you areas where you can more intentionally seek Him first.

....

....

....

....

....

....

....

Lord, cleanse my heart and open it to Your message today.

76

> Thomas said to Him, "Lord, we do not know where You are going, and how can we know the way?" Jesus said to him, "I am the way, the truth, and the life. No one comes to the Father except through Me."
>
> **JOHN 14:5-6**

All religion is not the same. All roads don't lead to God. But somehow we've bought the lie that we must put our arms around everyone and say, "You believe one way, and I believe another way, and your way is just as good as my way." As nice as this may sound, it is just not true.

There is only one way to worship God, and that's God's way. Jesus is not just a good way to Heaven. Jesus is not even the best way to Heaven. Jesus Christ is the only way to Heaven. This may sound very narrow-minded to some. But this truth comes straight from the Lord Jesus Himself. In John 14:6, Jesus said, "I am *the* way, *the* truth, and *the* life; and no one"—now listen to this—"no one comes to the Father except through Me" (emphasis added).

We find this truth again taught in Acts 4:12. The Bible says, "Nor is there salvation in any other, for there is no other name under heaven given among men by which we must be saved."

If Jesus Christ is not the only way to Heaven, Jesus Christ is none of the ways to Heaven. If Jesus Christ is not the only way to Heaven, Jesus is a faker, Jesus is a fraud, Jesus is a sham, Jesus is a charlatan because He claimed to be something that He was not. Our Savior is not a faker, a fraud, a sham, and a charlatan. He is the Son of God.

Why does this matter so much? Because every day you and I are surrounded by people who want to change, dilute, and broaden the way to Heaven. We must be kinder, more inclusive, and more tolerant. However, the Bible is crystal clear on this subject. In Matthew 7:13-14, we read, "Enter by the narrow gate; for wide is the gate and broad is the way that leads to destruction, and there are many who go in by it. Because narrow is the gate and difficult is the way which leads to life, and there are few who find it."

APPLICATION

Have you ever had a conversation about which roads lead to Heaven? How did it go? What did you discuss?

....

....

....

....

....

In your opinion, do you believe that Jesus is the only way to Heaven? Why or why not?

....

....

....

....

....

Why don't you talk the issue over with God today?

....

....

....

....

....

....

....

Open my heart to understand more about the power of praise today.

77

> And now, here are the people of Ammon, Moab, and Mount Seir—whom You would not let Israel invade when they came out of the land of Egypt, but they turned from them and did not destroy them—here they are, rewarding us by coming to throw us out of Your possession which You have given us to inherit. O our God, will You not judge them? For we have no power against this great multitude that is coming against us; nor do we know what to do, but our eyes are upon You.
>
> **2 CHRONICLES 20:10-12**

What does praise do? When we praise the Lord, what happens. Praise infuses the energy of God and praise confuses the enemies of God. There's something about praise that sends the enemy into consternation and confusion. There's a pattern in the Bible that when God's people begin to praise Him, when God's people say, "Our eyes are upon You," God sends confusion into the camp of the enemy.

I could take my Bible and show you four or five instances where this precise thing happened, where people began to trust God, look to God, praise God, and the enemy turned on himself and destroyed himself.

If you are in the middle of a problem, begin to praise God. We do this because God says in 2 Chronicles 20:15, "The battle is not yours, but it's God's." But you are going to have to take part in the battle. Your job in the battle is to praise. You can't hide out until the battle is over and then offer your praise. Instead, you must start singing and praising Him right now—right in the middle of the fight.

Perhaps you don't feel like you have the strength or courage to sing. But you must! That is the ultimate faith when we begin to praise God before we see the answer to our prayers. Praising in advance is our way of saying, "God, we don't know how You're going to do it. That's none of our business to know. But, God, You're bigger than this problem. And, therefore, I praise You."

APPLICATION

Have you ever thought about the power of praise? Why do you think praise is so powerful and effective—especially in battle?

....

....

....

....

....

Think about the most challenging situation in your life right now. What might happen if you started praising God during this trial?

....

....

....

....

....

As you pray today, praise God that He is mighty to save. Praise Him in advance of the victories that you need to see. You can write your praises in the space below.

....

....

....

....

....

....

....

Lord, speak to my heart as I read today.

78

> God, who at various times and in various ways spoke in time past to the fathers by the prophets, has in these last days spoken to us by His Son, whom He has appointed heir of all things, through whom also He made the worlds; who being the brightness of His glory and the express image of His person, and upholding all things by the word of His power, when He had by Himself purged our sins, sat down at the right hand of the Majesty on high, having become so much better than the angels, as He has by inheritance obtained a more excellent name than they.
>
> **HEBREWS 1:1-4**

H. G. Wells, the noted and famous historian, wrote in his outlines of history about the ten greatest men of all time. Number one on his list was Jesus Christ. However, Jesus Christ does not belong on anybody's list. He's not Jesus the great. You can talk about Alexander the Great. You can talk about Peter the Great; you can talk about Charlemagne the Great, but not Jesus the great. He is Jesus, the One and Only. He is in a class by Himself. Often, we want to say that Jesus was the first among men. That is not the case. He is God's unique and Only Begotten Son. He is our singular Savior. He is our superior Savior, and that's what I want us to think about.

You see, Jesus is unique among all of the so-called religious leaders. Buddha, Mohammed, and Confucius were all religious leaders, but let me tell you what all of these have in common. You can take them out of their teachings and still have their teachings. You can remove them from their religion and still have their religion. You can take Buddha out of Buddhism and still have Buddhism. You can take Mohammed out of Islam and still have Islam. You can take Confucius out of Confucianism and still have that system of thought.

But you can't take Christ out of Christianity and still have Christianity. Indeed, Christianity is not a code, not a cause, not a creed, not a church, but Christ. It is a vital relationship with the Lord Jesus Christ.

APPLICATION

What makes Jesus special and unique? How is He different from other religious leaders such as Buddha, Mohammed, and Confucius?

....

....

....

....

....

How has Jesus changed your life? How are you different because you know the Christ of Christianity?

....

....

....

....

Take a few moments and thank God for the person of Jesus.

....

....

....

....

....

....

Open my eyes to understand as I read today.

79

God, who at various times and in various ways spoke in time past to the fathers by the prophets, has in these last days spoken to us by His Son, whom He has appointed heir of all things, through whom also He made the worlds; who being the brightness of His glory and the express image of His person, and upholding all things by the word of His power, when He had by Himself purged our sins, sat down at the right hand of the Majesty on high, having become so much better than the angels, as He has by inheritance obtained a more excellent name than they.

HEBREWS 1:1-4

A man bought a house and he wanted to have the house remodeled. An architect was brought in to discuss the renovations. One of the things that the homeowner wanted to do was to remove an odd-looking cabinet that was awkwardly placed in the middle of the house. The architect refused to remove the cabinet. The homeowner offered him more money to make the changes. That's when the architect explained the problem. He told the homeowner, "The house is resting on that cabinet. And if I remove the cabinet, the entire house will come down."

This is the truth about Christianity as well. If you take the person of Jesus Christ out of the center of Christianity, the entire "house" of Christianity collapses like a house of cards. Jesus is foundational. Jesus is fundamental to Christianity. He is unique. None can compare with Him among the sons of men.

Think with me and rejoice with me about our superlative Savior. I don't know if you know Him and love Him, but I pray that you do. If you don't know Him and love Him, it is my prayer that the message of this devotional will inculcate in your heart a hunger to know our wonderful Savior. You can come to learn more about Jesus. You can develop a greater love for Him. However, you can never learn or love anything better than Jesus. He is the best, and there's nothing that can compare.

APPLICATION

Have you ever thought about what holds up your home or apartment? What is at the center of your place of residence? What gives it stability?

....

....

....

....

Why is Jesus so essential to Christianity? Why is He the best, the One without comparison?

....

....

....

....

Take a few moments to pray and thank God for the stability that Jesus offers to your faith.

....

....

....

....

....

Lord, help me to grasp more about Jesus as I read today.

80

God, who at various times and in various ways spoke in time past to the fathers by the prophets, has in these last days spoken to us by His Son, whom He has appointed heir of all things, through whom also He made the worlds; who being the brightness of His glory and the express image of His person, and upholding all things by the word of His power, when He had by Himself purged our sins, sat down at the right hand of the Majesty on high, having become so much better than the angels, as He has by inheritance obtained a more excellent name than they.

HEBREWS 1:1-4

Years ago, I had the privilege of pastoring a church near the Kennedy Space Center in Cape Canaveral. On several occasions, I got to watch the giant Saturn missiles as they launched astronauts into space. It was an awesome thing to see. That missile, three hundred and sixty-five feet tall, was taller than a giant skyscraper. A button would be pushed, and the rockets would begin to rumble. The earth would shake, and the rockets would slowly start to move as onlookers cheered. To lift off would take seven and a half million pounds of thrust.

Do you know how much that is? If you can imagine a string of diesel locomotives stretched from New York to Chicago, all of them revving their engines up at the same time, that's how much power is in that one missile as it's trying to launch a few people into orbit.

As you think about how God put universes into orbit, you can also imagine His great power and might. Consider how our God flung stars into orbit and holds them there by the word of His power. God made it all and He holds it all together. The Bible says that nothing was made apart from Jesus. He is the power of creation and the possessor of creation. The Bible also says he is appointed heir of all things. It all belongs to Jesus.

APPLICATION

Have you ever seen a rocket take off (in person or on television)? What was it like? What impressed you most?

_____

_____

_____

_____

How hard do you suppose it was for God to fling the stars into space? How would you describe the power and might of God?

_____

_____

_____

_____

Take a moment to praise God for His power and might today. Write out your prayer below.

_____

_____

_____

_____

_____

Lord, reveal to me any ways that I don't trust You as I should.

81

> God, who at various times and in various ways spoke in time past to the fathers by the prophets, has in these last days spoken to us by His Son, whom He has appointed heir of all things, through whom also He made the worlds; who being the brightness of His glory and the express image of His person, and upholding all things by the word of His power, when He had by Himself purged our sins, sat down at the right hand of the Majesty on high, having become so much better than the angels, as He has by inheritance obtained a more excellent name than they.
>
> **HEBREWS 1:1-4**

Often, people ask me—what's this world coming to? That's easy. It's coming to Jesus. He's the heir of all things. All things were made by Him and for Him and they're all coming to Jesus.

That's why we are careful who we follow. Following Jesus is the best choice. Jesus is inheriting the Earth. It belongs to the Lord Jesus Christ. It will all come to Him and He will rule as King of kings, as Lord of lords. This mighty Universe and this planet Earth upon which we live belongs to the Lord. He's the power of creation. He is the possessor of creation. And He is the preserver of creation.

Hebrews 1:3 tells us that Jesus is, "upholding all things by the word of His power." What keeps everything from disintegrating? What holds those mighty stars in orbit and mathematical precision? Jesus. The Bible says by Him all things consist. He's the glue of the galaxies. He's the one who holds it all together.

There are times when scientists worry that we are going to have an atomic chain reaction. Our world is going to be turned into a glob of molten steel according to some of these experts. They worry about things like global warming and other ecological events. However, the Bible teaches us that none of these things can happen unless Jesus allows it. He is the one who upholds all things by the word of His power. The future of our world is ultimately under His care and control.

APPLICATION

Have you ever thought about the fact that Jesus is in control of our world and the preserver of all creation? How does this make you feel?

....

....

....

....

When you think about the fears of the scientists and those concerned about global warming, how does Jesus' power counter those fears and concerns? Do you trust Him to be the glue of the galaxies and the glue of your life? Why or why not?

....

....

....

....

Take a few moments to pray about those things that concern you today. Invite Jesus to give you a greater faith in His power.

....

....

....

....

....

Lord, help me to agree with You as I read today.

82

> So when they saw Him, they were amazed; and His mother said to Him, "Son, why have You done this to us? Look, Your father and I have sought You anxiously." And He said to them, "Why did you seek Me? Did you not know that I must be about My Father's business?"
>
> **LUKE 2:48-49**

Do you remember the first spoken words of the Lord Jesus recorded in the Bible? They are from today's verses. Jesus said, "I must be about My Father's business." Jesus was always about His Father's business. He commenced His Father's business and He stayed with His Father's business until He could bow His head upon that cross and say, "It is finished" (John 19:30).

Often, the people around us are asking so many questions of us. What are we going to do about all of the problems in our world? What are we going to do about the overcrowded prisons? What are we going to do about poverty? What are we going to do about rape? What are we going to do about murder? What are we going to do? The reason we never solve these problems (and so many more) is that we don't see the real problem.

What is the real problem? Sociologists say it's a cultural lag. Psychologists call it an emotional disturbance. The philosopher calls it irrational behavior. The Communist calls it a class struggle. The humanist calls it a human weakness. The criminologist calls it anti-social conduct. Yet, the Bible calls it sin. And there's only one answer for sin. The answer is Jesus, who by Himself purged our sins. You can never handle the sin problem until you settle things with the Son of God, Jesus Christ.

Years ago, Sandra and Andraé Crouch wrote a song about this very subject, "Jesus Is the Answer." The lyrics seem so appropriate here. *"Jesus is the answer for the world today. Above Him there's no other, Jesus is the way. Jesus is the answer for the world today. Above Him there's no other, Jesus is the way."*

APPLICATION

What did Jesus mean when He said He must be about His Father's business?

....

....

....

....

Do you agree that Jesus is the answer for our world today? Why or why not?

....

....

....

....

As you pray today, ask God to give you a greater love and appreciation for Jesus.

....

....

....

....

....

....

....

Lord, open my eyes to grasp the truth as I read today.

83

> For God so loved the world that He gave His only
> begotten Son, that whoever believes in Him should
> not perish but have everlasting life. For God did not
> send His Son into the world to condemn the world,
> but that the world through Him might be saved.
>
> **JOHN 3:16-17**

Pastor Robert G. Lee faithfully served Bellevue Baptist Church in Memphis, Tennessee, for several years. He loved to talk about Jesus. Dr. Lee often shared that Jesus is literature's loftiest ideal. He said that Jesus is philosophy's highest personality and that He is the fundamental doctrine of theological criticism (critical analysis to understand and explain the Bible). Additionally, He said that Jesus is the ultimate answer to the emptiness of religion.

Do you know Jesus? Has he ever come into your heart? Have you ever received Him as your Lord and Savior? Have you ever said, "Yes, I know that I know that He lives in me"? I want to tell you that Jesus Christ is a bright, living reality in my heart. Jesus Christ is as real to me as these clothes that I'm wearing. He's as real to me as my relationships with my wife and children.

Many mornings, I wake up with thoughts of Jesus on my mind. He is personal to me. I want to know Him more, and I want you to know Him. Is Jesus Christ real to you? Is He personal to you? Do you know what the message of this devotional is today? This message is the Holy Spirit bringing to you the hope and truth of Jesus. I want to tell you today that the Holy Spirit is God's dove to bring a message from Heaven to tell you that God loves you.

Jesus wants to save you. The Spirit has come from Heaven to bear to you this message, that Jesus is the superlative Savior. He is Lord of lords and King of kings. If you will receive Him, according to Isaiah 1:18, "Though your sins are like scarlet, they shall be as white as snow." And even now, God's dear Spirit is at the windowsill of your heart. Open it up. Receive Him. Trust Him. He'll save you. He will save you right now.

APPLICATION

Have you seen Jesus fill the void and the emptiness in someone else's life? What took place?

....

....

....

....

How about in your own life? Has Jesus saved you? If so, how did you come to Christ? If not, why not invite Him to save you today? The Bible tells us in Romans 10:13, "whoever calls on the name of the LORD shall be saved."

....

....

....

....

Why not take a few moments to talk these things over with the Lord? If you are saved, thank Jesus for your salvation. If not, today would be a great day to invite Him to save you. Tell God you're a sinner, you want to be forgiven, and you trust Jesus' finished work on the cross.

....

....

....

....

....

Lord, show me any ways in which I am not experiencing liberty right now.

> Now the Lord is the Spirit; and where the Spirit of the Lord is, there is liberty.
>
> **2 CORINTHIANS 3:17**

Years ago, I read a story about the tyrant king of Syracuse. This king called a blacksmith before his throne and asked him to put on a demonstration. The king asked the blacksmith to forge a chain before his throne. All of the necessary tools were brought in, molten metal, an anvil, a hammer, and everything that was needed to make the chain.

The blacksmith, who was known as the best in the kingdom, began to forge a chain. Hammering and working away, he created a great chain for the king. As he presented the chain to the tyrant king, he was asked if his chain was strong. The blacksmith replied, "Sire, you could put a team of horses on either end of the chain, and they'd not be able to snap that chain." Then, according to the story, the tyrant of Syracuse said, "Guards, take the blacksmith. Bind him in that chain and cast him in the dungeon."

When I read that story, I thought how much like Satan this tyrant king was. Satan takes the very chains that we have forged and he binds us in these chains and keeps us in the dungeon of despair. But the Bible says the Holy Spirit wants to break those chains asunder. The Holy Spirit wants to give us the glorious liberty that belongs to the children of God. God's Spirit wants us to sing with liberty, preach with liberty, testify with liberty, live with liberty, give with liberty, and die with liberty. We were never meant to be bound by chains.

Truly, where the Spirit of the Lord is, there is glorious liberty. However, so many people today do not enjoy true freedom in their lives. They were set free when they invited Jesus into their lives, but they returned to their chains. I wonder, is there something in your life right now that binds you or holds you back. Is there possibly one little chain that you are dragging around with you? This is not how God intended us to live. "Where the Spirit of the Lord is, there is liberty."

APPLICATION

What did you think about the story of the tyrannical king in today's devotion? How is he like Satan?

....

....

....

....

Is there anything in your life that binds you or holds you back? Is there possibly one little chain that you are dragging around with you? Why not ask the Spirit of God to free you up again?

....

....

....

....

Take a few moments to pray about any "chains" in your life that may have taken hold. Invite God to bring freedom, healing, and restoration.

....

....

....

....

....

....

Teach me, Lord, more about the Spirit as I read and study today.

85

> If you love Me, keep My commandments. And I will pray the
> Father, and He will give you another Helper, that He may
> abide with you forever—the Spirit of truth, whom the world
> cannot receive, because it neither sees Him nor knows
> Him; but you know Him, for He dwells with you and will be
> in you. I will not leave you orphans; I will come to you.
>
> **JOHN 14:15-18**

Who is the Holy Spirit? Many people do not understand that the Holy Spirit is the Lord. They speak of the Holy Spirit as an it, or as a thing. Moreover, there is a false cult that calls the Holy Spirit God's active force. But they do not think of Him as a person.

Further, they think that the idea of the triune God, God the Father, and God the Son, and God the Holy Spirit is some sort of a pagan, mythological, or philosophical idea that men have cooked up. This causes them to deny the personality of the Holy Spirit. But the Holy Spirit is a person, just as Jesus is a person, and just as God is a person. It's so important that you understand this. People will not worship an influence. Rather, people worship a person, and the Holy Spirit is a person. When Dwight L. Moody was a new believer, he was told by an old saint to honor the Holy Spirit. Moody did that, and God made him a great evangelist.

Similarly, we must learn to honor the Holy Spirit because He's a person. This is important in our worship and our service to God. If we think of the Holy Spirit as a thing or some sort of impersonal force, we may see Him as something we "get." People go around talking about "getting the Holy Ghost." When you understand the proper doctrine of the Holy Spirit, you don't talk about "getting the Holy Ghost." You talk about the Holy Spirit having you. You don't possess it; He possesses you. When you realize that He wants to possess you, that leads to humility and great usefulness. Knowing the Spirit enables us to worship and to serve with more passion, more usefulness, and more wisdom.

APPLICATION

What do you know and understand about the Holy Spirit? What does He do?

_____

_____

_____

_____

_____

How have you personally viewed the Holy Spirit? Who is He to you?

_____

_____

_____

_____

Why not pray over these matters today as you close your devotional time? Invite God to teach you more about the Spirit. You may want to write your prayer below.

_____

_____

_____

_____

_____

_____

_____

Lord, help me to grasp more about the Holy Spirit today.

—— 86 ——

> But God has revealed them to us through His Spirit. For the Spirit searches all things, yes, the deep things of God. For what man knows the things of a man except the spirit of the man which is in him? Even so no one knows the things of God except the Spirit of God.
>
> **1 CORINTHIANS 2:10-11**

What does the Holy Spirit do? How does the Bible describe and define the Spirit? According to today's verses, the Spirit knows about God and us. He knows, understands, and imparts great wisdom to us. In 1 Corinthians 2:11, we read, "Even so no one knows the things of God except the Spirit of God." The Spirit of God has great knowledge and understanding.

Additionally, the Spirit of God has an active will. When the Bible is talking about spiritual gifts in 1 Corinthians 12:11, "But one and the same Spirit works all these things, distributing to each one individually as He wills." The Spirit of God has a will and distributes gifts based on that will.

Also, the Spirit has emotions. In Romans 15:30a, we read where Paul speaks of the Spirit, "Now I beg you, brethren, through the Lord Jesus Christ, and through the love of the Spirit." Did you know that the Holy Spirit loves? For those that believe the Spirit is a thing, this would be confusing. Things can't show and feel love. A thing can't love. A Chevrolet can't love. Television can't love. A microphone can't love. A watch can't love. Electricity cannot love. The Holy Spirit is a person full of love.

Often, we speak of the love of God the Father. We will also speak of the love of Jesus. Also, we can thank and praise the Holy Spirit for His love. What if today we were to say something like this to the Spirit, "Oh, blessed Spirit of God, how I love you! I would be in Hell were it not for you. Thank you for loving me and seeking me out. I'm so grateful that you found me and revealed to me the sacrifice of Jesus on Calvary. Thank you for making Jesus real to me."

APPLICATION

In your understanding, what does the Spirit of God do? Describe Him in your own words.

....

....

....

....

....

Is God's Spirit real to you? If so, how? If not, why not?

....

....

....

....

As you close, why not pray and thank the Spirit for leading you to Jesus? Thank Him for convicting and convincing you!

....

....

....

....

....

....

....

Lord, show me any ways in which I resist the Spirit in my life.

87

> You stiff-necked and uncircumcised in heart and ears! You always resist the Holy Spirit; as your fathers did, so do you. Which of the prophets did your fathers not persecute? And they killed those who foretold the coming of the Just One, of whom you now have become the betrayers and murderers, who have received the law by the direction of angels and have not kept it.
>
> **ACTS 7:51-53**

In the early days of American history, a red-headed Virginian stood up one day, Patrick Henry, and said, "I know not what course others may take, but as for me, give me liberty or give me death." People stopped saying that a few generations back. They just started saying, "Give me liberty." And now, we've raised a generation that just says, "Give me."

People are not as interested in liberty today. However, we are promised the liberating power of the Holy Spirit. To enjoy that power, we must understand an important thing about the Spirit. The Holy Spirit must be the residing Spirit. Truly, there are only two things we can do with the Holy Spirit. Either we resist Him or we receive Him.

In the Early Church, there was a man named Stephen who preached Jesus to the people. Acts 7 is a lengthy sermon preached by Stephen in which he told the crowd about the crucified Lord. His words shook the people to the core of their beings as he said, "You stiff-necked and uncircumcised in heart and ears! You always resist the Holy Spirt; as your fathers did, so do you" (Acts 7:51).

Truly, the Holy Spirit may be resisted. He is a gentle dove, and He's not going to force His way upon anyone's life. And people can be rebellious. They can be hard-hearted. They can be stiff-necked, and they can say no to God's Holy Spirit. Indeed, when these people heard Stephen's message, they picked up stones and hurled the stones at him to silence him. Resisting the prompting of the Spirit, they turned on God's messenger and killed him for speaking the truth.

APPLICATION

Have you also noticed how our society has moved from, "Give me liberty or give me death," to just, "Give me"? Why do you think this is true or false?

....

....

....

....

Do you ever feel like you resist the promptings of the Holy Spirit? How do things turn out for you when you resist Him?

....

....

....

....

As you pray today, invite the Spirit to continue to lead you and speak to you. Tell Him how much you want to receive Him rather than resist Him.

....

....

....

....

....

....

Father, teach me any ways in which my speech quenches your Spirit.

88

And do not grieve the Holy Spirit of God, by whom you were sealed for the day of redemption.

EPHESIANS 4:30

Are you and I letting the Holy Spirit have His way in our lives? Does He reign? Have we given Him control of our lives? Unfortunately, some people know the Holy Spirit as a resident, but they do not know Him as president. With some people, He has come in to abide but not to preside. Other people have the Holy Spirit within them, but the Holy Spirit does not have them completely. The Holy Spirit is dormant in their lives, but He is not dominant in their lives.

Second Corinthians 3:17 teaches us that "...where the Spirit of the Lord is, there is liberty." Are you experiencing that liberty? Did you know that you can have the Holy Spirit living within you, but not controlling you? The Bible teaches us to be filled with the Spirit, to allow Him to completely take over. However, sometimes we limit His filling. We push Him away. How do we do this?

In Ephesians 4:30, we are encouraged not to, "grieve the Holy Spirit of God." What does it mean to grieve the Spirit? To grieve the Spirit is to allow unconfessed sin to take over in our lives. One way we do this is with our speech. Ephesians 4:25 mentions this, "Therefore, putting away lying, 'Let each one of you speak truth with his neighbor,' for we are members of one another." We are also reminded to be careful how we speak in Ephesians 5:3, "But fornication and all uncleanness or covetousness, let it not even be named among you, as is fitting for saints."

We grieve the Holy Spirit when we open our mouths and the filth and the stench of the sewer spills out. We take the name of Jesus Christ in vain. We tell dirty, smutty, off-color jokes, and the Holy Spirit within us is broken-hearted. He's just as hurt as your saintly mother or grandmother would be if she were to hear you curse and blaspheme your earthly father. Truly, you will never know true freedom until you learn not to grieve the Holy Spirit.

APPLICATION

Why do you think so many Christians treat the Holy Spirit as a resident but not as the president of their lives? Why is this so easy to do?

....

....

....

....

Do you ever grieve the Spirit of God? What about the jokes you tell and the way you speak? Is there anything God wants you to correct, change, or edit in the way you talk?

....

....

....

....

Take a few moments to pray over these things. Ask God if there is anything He'd like you to change. You may want to write out a prayer in the space below.

....

....

....

....

....

....

Open my heart to learn new things as I read today.

> And do not be drunk with wine, in which is dissipation;
> but be filled with the Spirit, speaking to one another
> in psalms and hymns and spiritual songs, singing
> and making melody in your heart to the Lord.
>
> **EPHESIANS 5:18-19**

What does it mean to be filled with the Spirit? The Bible says to be, "filled with the Spirit." So, what does that look like? Notice that the Bible doesn't tell us to be filled *by* the Spirit. He doesn't just fill me up with all sorts of goodies. He comes in. Be filled *with* the Spirit.

Do you remember the temple of the Jewish people? There were three parts: the Holy of Holies, the inner court, and the outer court. The Holy of Holies represents your spirit, the inner court is your soul, and the outer court is your body. When you get saved, the Holy Spirit comes to live in the Holy of Holies. He resides in your spirit. But to be truly filled with the Spirit, you allow Him to move into the inner court and the outer court of your life, represented by your soul and your body.

When a person is Spirit-filled, the Holy Spirit not only dwells within his spirit, but He dwells within a person's mind, psyche, soul, and emotions. Then, the Spirit is manifested in a person's body. This is done through faith to his eyes, his lips, his tongue, his hands. All that he has is motivated by the Spirit. The Spirit speaks to the soul, and the soul drives the body. A person does not simply possess the Holy Spirit; the Holy Spirit possesses him.

When this happens in your life, you are on the verge of the most glorious liberty that a person can have. You'll enjoy unbelievable liberty to stand for Christ, to speak for Christ, and to serve others. Also, you'll have the liberty to avoid what you shouldn't do and to do what you should. Living filled with the Spirit will free you to live to your fullest potential, expressing Jesus through all that you do. Your entire existence will manifest the person of Jesus Christ.

APPLICATION

In your own words, how would you explain being full of the Spirit to someone else? Why does this filling of the Spirit matter in our lives?

....

....

....

....

As you evaluate your own life, would you say that you are living a life that is full of the Holy Spirit? Why or why not? Is there anything that you'd like to do differently?

....

....

....

....

Take a few moments to pray about these matters. Talk to God about these things.

....

....

....

....

....

Lord, bolster and strengthen my faith and courage today.

> Now therefore, fear the LORD, serve Him in sincerity and in truth, and put away the gods which your fathers served on the other side of the River and in Egypt. Serve the LORD! And if it seems evil to you to serve the LORD, choose for yourselves this day whom you will serve, whether the gods which your fathers served that were on the other side of the River, or the gods of the Amorites, in whose land you dwell. But as for me and my house, we will serve the LORD.
>
> **JOSHUA 24:14-15**

Can we worship God through our service? The word "serve" literally means to do homage, to worship. This doesn't mean that you go around doing things for God. It means to worship Him, to love Him, to bow before Him with all of your heart. And what is that worship to be? We are told to "serve him in sincerity." The word "sincere" means to be without blemish. This term was used of sacrificed animals that were to be whole and complete, lacking nothing.

What does this all mean for you and me? I'm to present my body a living sacrifice, holy, acceptable unto God. It's to be a sincere, daily, continual service. Additionally, I'm to, "Serve him in sincerity and in truth" (Joshua 24:14). There is no substitute for truth nor for sincerity. If you worship the Lord in sincerity without truth, you'll be a fanatic. If you worship the Lord in truth and not in sincerity, you'll be a legalist. But if you worship the Lord and serve the Lord in sincerity and truth; you'll be a beautiful Christian.

Finally, we are to worship steadfastly. In Joshua 24:15, Joshua says, "We will serve the LORD." Willfully and willingly, we will choose to serve the Lord, no matter what anyone or everyone else chooses. I believe that the closer we get to the end of the age, the more we are going to have to stand alone. Noah stood alone and was called a bigot and a fool, no doubt. Elijah stood alone before 450 prophets of Baal. Amos stood alone before the king's court. You also may have to stand alone. It's time to declare your faith as Joshua did.

APPLICATION

What are some ways we can worship God through our service? What does this look like when it is lived out?

....

....

....

....

....

Have you ever found yourself having to stand alone, to stand up for what was right? Share your story below.

....

....

....

....

....

As you pray today, invite God to fill you with the most courageous faith you've ever had.

....

....

....

....

....

....

Come to Jesus.

For all have sinned and fall short of the glory of God.
ROMANS 3:23

Believe on the Lord Jesus Christ, and you will be saved...
ACTS 16:31

If we confess our sins, He is faithful and just to forgive us
our sins and to cleanse us from all unrighteousness.
1 JOHN 1:9

...if any man be in Christ, he is a new creature: old things
are passed away; behold, all things are become new.
2 CORINTHIANS 5:17

Therefore whoever confesses Me before men, him I will
also confess before My Father Who is in heaven.
MATTHEW 10:32

Then he said to Jesus, "Lord, remember me when You come
into Your kingdom." And Jesus said to him, "Assuredly,
I say to you, today you will be with Me in Paradise."
LUKE 23:42-43

L uke 23 tells of the salvation of the thief who was crucified next to Jesus. This thief was given more in a moment than he had stolen in a lifetime. He went straight to Heaven from that cross (see 2 Corinthians 5:8). Jesus wants you to join Him in Paradise, too! All it takes is a simple, sincere act of faith, just as this man demonstrated. Like him, you must see yourself as a sinner and understand that there is a holy God whose wrath burns against sin. You must recognize Jesus as the sinless, sovereign, saving Christ who died in your place. Then willingly turn from your sin to Jesus and pray, "Lord, remember me."

Right now, you can put your faith where God has placed your sins—on Jesus. You might pray something like this:

> *Dear God, I'm a sinner and my sin deserves judgment. I know You love me and You want to save me. Jesus, You paid my sin debt with Your blood on the cross. You died and rose again that I might have life. I lift my hand of faith now to receive Your gift of grace. Come into my heart, forgive my sin and save me. You're now my Lord, my Savior, my God and my friend. I stand on Your Word and receive it by faith, and that settles it. Give me the courage to step out in obedience, Lord, and show my faith publicly. Begin making me the person You want me to be. In Your Name I pray, Amen.*

If you just prayed to receive Christ, we'd love to hear from you so that we can provide you with free resources to help you grow in your new faith. Please let us know by going to **lwf.org/discover-jesus**, scrolling down the page and clicking on *I Believe*.

We also want to encourage you to take the next step by finding a Bible-believing church where you can openly confess your faith in Christ through believer's baptism. Pray about joining with a local body of believers who can welcome you into their fellowship and help you to grow in your newfound faith. Stay in God's Word, continuing to hear from Him each day, and learning to live a victorious life of wonder and worship!

The greatest miracle is the salvation of a soul. No other miracle cost God anything. When God made this world, He simply spoke and it was so.

When He healed a blind man, caused a lame person to walk, or cast demons from someone...all He had to do was say so, and they were healed.

But to save a soul, God had to hang His dear Son on a cross. The only time God went to any difficulty to do anything was Calvary.

The greatest miracle is the healing of a sin-sick soul.

ADRIAN ROGERS

Additional Notes

Adrian Rogers, one of America's most respected Bible teachers, faithfully preached the Word of God for 53 years—32 of those years as senior pastor of the historic Bellevue Baptist Church near Memphis, Tennessee.

In 1987, Pastor Rogers founded Love Worth Finding Ministries to communicate the Gospel of Jesus Christ.

Today his messages are broadcast around the globe digitally and through radio and television. His work is being translated into a growing collection of languages.

Love Worth Finding touches millions the world over with the profound truth of the Gospel, simply stated, all with the goal of bringing people to Jesus and helping them grow in the faith.

WILL YOU SUPPORT LOVE WORTH FINDING?

This ministry is funded primarily by gifts from Christians committed to sharing God's Word with lost and hurting people from all walks of life.

———

If this resource has been a help to you, please consider joining with us to bless others with the Gospel of Jesus Christ.

lwf.org/give

LOVEWORTHFINDING®
WITH ADRIAN ROGERS

PO Box 38300   Memphis TN 38183-0300   (901) 382-7900

Additional Titles by
Adrian Rogers, Joyce Rogers &
Love Worth Finding Ministries
Published by Innovo Publishing LLC

1. *25 Days of Anticipation: Jesus . . . The Fulfillment of Every Heart's Longing*
2. *A Family Christmas Treasury*
3. *Adrianisms: The Collected Wit and Wisdom of Adrian Rogers*
4. *Believe in Miracles but Trust in Jesus*
5. *Discover Jesus: The Author and Finisher of our Faith*
6. *Foundations for Our Faith: A 3-Volume Bible Study of Romans*
7. *God's Hidden Treasures*
8. *God's Wisdom is Better than Gold*
9. *Good Morning, Lord: Starting Each Day with the Risen Lord (a 365 Day Devotional)*
10. *His Story: God's Purpose and Plans from Genesis to Revelation*
11. *Revelation Study Guide (2 Volumes)*
12. *Seeing Jesus in Unexpected Places: A Fascinating Look at the Old Testament Tabernacle*
13. *Standing for Light and Truth: Living with Integrity to Shine God's Light in a World Going Dim*
14. *The Music of Marriage*
15. *The Passion of Christ and the Purpose of Life*
16. *The Power of His Presence*

* BY JOYCE ROGERS *

17. *Therefore, I Hope In Him*
18. *Chosen to be a Minister's Wife*
19. *Behold*